O

RIDING MASTERCLASS

Edited by **Jo Weeks**

D&C
David and Charles

A DAVID & CHARLES BOOK

First published in the UK in 2008
This paperback edition first published in the UK in 2009

Layout and design © David & Charles
Source material courtesy of *Horse & Rider magazine* © DJ Murphy Ltd.
Except photos on pages 4, 20–24, 26–27, 30–33, 144 (right) and 145
(top) © Kit Houghton and pages 6–7 and 53 © Bob Langrish

David & Charles is an F+W Media Inc. company
4700 East Galbraith Road
Cincinnati, OH 45236

A catalogue record for this book is available from the British Library.

ISBN-13: 978-0-7153-2916-0 paperback
ISBN-10: 0-7153-2916-2 paperback

Printed in China by SNP Leefung
for David & Charles
Brunel House   Newton Abbot   Devon

Commissioning Editor: Jane Trollope
Editorial Manager: Emily Pitcher
Assistant Editor: Emily Rae
Designer: Jodie Lystor
Production Controller: Beverley Richardson

Visit our website at www.davidandcharles.co.uk

David & Charles books are available from all good bookshops;
alternatively you can contact our Orderline on 0870 9908222
or write to us at FREEPOST EX2 110, D&C Direct, Newton Abbot,
TQ12 4ZZ (no stamp required UK only); US customers call
800-289-0963 and Canadian customers call 800-840-5220.

CONTENTS

Introduction

How wonderful it would be to be able to call up one of the equestrian world's most eminent trainers for advice, or to arrange a lesson at a moments notice! Very few of us have the connections or the budget to make this a reality, but we can immerse ourselves in the collection of lessons offered in the following pages.

These are real lessons, with real riders and their horses, and as such they offer genuine insight into dealing with everyday issues. You can expect to find solutions to the problems that you might experience in your own schooling sessions provided by top instructors and international competitors from the worlds of dressage and eventing. Begin by watching the masters at work as they describe their own approach to a variety of aspects of schooling, before following the lessons. Finally see how you can improve your test results and get more from your riding.

It might be the closest thing to a personal lesson with your favourite trainer that you can currently aspire to, but let this book be the beginning of better riding for you and better schooling for your horse. Whatever your goals and expectations, you will find so much in *Riding Masterclass* to inspire and guide you.

THE MASTERS

Learning how to perform a variety of controlled athletic movements gives your horse some of the mental and physical skills he needs to survive in our world. This might sound exaggerated, but besides enabling him to do well in dressage tests, they teach him how to carry himself in balance and self-control while doing everything you ask of him. This will give him confidence in all areas of his life since he can trust you to communicate your needs clearly and simply.

   In this section, well-known riders and trainers go through a selection of the most important school movements. They share techniques that they have acquired through years of experience, pass on tips for how best to explain what is required to the horse, and describe what to do if things don't go according to plan. As your horse becomes well versed in these movements, he can begin to make deductions about what you are asking whenever you start to teach him something new, so each new movement can be learnt more quickly and more easily. Most importantly, good schooling helps a horse to remain calm and to listen to you whenever he is unsure.

Holistic schooling – Richard Davison

I strongly believe in holistic training for horses, and riders – that is, looking at every aspect of the horse's life, and not just how he performs. A living creature can only perform at his best if he's happy and comfortable, and with horses you have to look at everything from stable management, general health and diet, to exercise routine and tack. These things also need fine-tuning from time to time, so find out what's best for your horse and monitor his performance. It doesn't matter what age, shape, size or level of experience you and your horse are – these techniques are suitable for anyone.

> **THE HORSES**
>
> *Richard Davison* talks about holistic schooling and demonstrates his work with two of his horses – *Hiscox Kaluchi*, a Holsteiner by Lucky Champ, and *Hiscox Chalifas*, a Trakehner.

Before I start warming up my horses, I often feed them a sugar lump, a mint or a piece of apple. This encourages them to chew the bit and be more relaxed in the mouth

Warming up

I warm up on a half-long rein, which means the horse has freedom in his neck but is stretching forwards and down, so he's also working his topline. This is the length of rein my horses hack out on, too. The first aim is to achieve flexibility and suppleness, so ride some large circles in all three paces, until you're happy that your horse feels mentally and physically relaxed. I find staying on a large circle is a good way to help the horse relax more. Bending his neck encourages stretching and discourages running off on the forehand. But move your circle around the school. A horse's state of mind (pysche) is what controls the relaxing or tensing of his muscles, so being relaxed mentally will also help relax him physically. I usually warm up for about 15 minutes, depending on the horse.

Avoid making any abrupt turns as you circle. It is important to give the horse plenty of warning that you're going to do something else, so let him know when you wish to make a downward transition, or change of rein, for example. This is what is meant by preparation – and it will ensure that his balance, rhythm and suppleness are maintained.

Richard gives Hiscox Kaluchi time to stretch and warm up his muscles on a half-long rein

---

LEG CONTROL

- If your horse starts off a bit sharp, a secure lower leg will help you stay secure in the saddle. A good way to improve your lower leg strength and position is to ride in jumping position with your stirrups at jump length and without reins, so you don't balance on the horse's mouth. (This is best done on a safe horse on the lunge.) Push down into your heel; if you find it hard to balance on your legs alone, hold a neckstrap. If being lunged isn't an option, then you can stretch your calf muscles by standing with the ball of your foot on the edge of a step and pushing down gently into your heel.
- I ride young horses in little spurs. Just because you wear spurs, it doesn't mean you have to use them, but it is important to have full control of your leg position – no wobbling. The whip I carry is short, so I don't catch the horse with it by mistake. With young horses I also recommend a neckstrap for rider safety.

A relaxed leg, in constant contact, is important for giving signals and receiving feedback from your horse – listen to this feedback so you know when to ask for more, or less

Transitions

I teach my horses transitions on the lunge first, so they learn to respond to my voice. Then, when I'm riding, I use the same voice commands but with a subtle rein aid, too. This way horses are taught to listen to very light rein aids right from the start. For upward transitions use a sharp tone, and for downward ones use a softer tone: for example, T…ROT to go up a gear and WO…AH to stop. Make your upward transitions exciting, full of energy, setting the horse alight, and downward ones calm and supple – but don't let your horse lose impulsion. I prefer not to take sitting trot before walking or cantering because it encourages hollowing. Also, why change anything before asking the horse for something new? It only gives him reason to tense up. However, staying in rising trot does make it harder for the rider to balance so for most it is better to establish a good sitting trot well before the transition. I school and even warm up for my Grand Prix tests in rising trot as it is more comfortable for the horse. Rise wherever you can in dressage tests.

Are you being consistent?

Mental association plays a big part in teaching horses how to make good transitions. If you work on the principle that every time you ride a transition your horse must stay on the bit, engage his hindlegs and offer the transition as soon as you ask, then he will soon learn what you expect from him. To do this successfully, though, you must not accept even one transition that isn't good. And if it's still not how you want it after 20 attempts, then could it be something you're doing – or not doing. Ask someone to watch you, if you're not sure.

Square exercise

I do this exercise with my young horses to help them with transitions, and they respond well to it. Mark out a square of about 15m (50ft) in a corner of the school using poles to make the two extra sides. Square poles are best as they won't roll.

Ride in working trot around the perimeter of your square – making sure you go into the corners (see p.15 for riding better corners) – and ask for a walk transition just before a corner. You may find the horse resists and hollows at first, but after a few attempts he should stay softer. This technique works because the horse slows down naturally as he approaches the corner, which means you don't need as much rein contact, and that means he has less rein pressure to resist against. Once he's offering decent transitions, ride the same exercise but don't actually walk. Move the horse on again before he offers walk – this is the preparation for a half-halt and helps to keep the horse's hindquarters engaged.

For power and brakes

If your car has good brakes you don't mind driving it with a bit of power, and it's the same with a horse. If your horse is a 'goer' (he wants to go everywhere at top speed), then this exercise will help to improve his braking system.

Go large around the arena, and as you come on to a long side, ask for medium trot. Ride to about halfway along the long side – just when your 'goer' is about to really rev up – and make a walk transition. Repeat this until your horse starts to anticipate the walk transition. If he's waiting for the command to walk, he won't want to stiffen and run.

I always start to teach medium trot on the long side of the school so that if the horse has any memories of training difficulties these are not associated with the diagonal, where he has to perform medium trot in a test. I only progress to the diagonal when the horse is balanced and fluent on the long side.

TRANSITION TIPS

- Lighten your seat and bring your upper body slightly forwards during an upward transition.
- For downward ones, bring your upper body into a more upright position.
- Use the lightest aids possible, and only ask more if your horse doesn't respond first time round.

Richard rides rising trot whenever possible, to enable his horses to use their back freely. This is Hiscox Chalifas

To improve canter

Your horse needs to learn to stay in the pace you put him in until you ask otherwise. And there is no exception to this rule, even in canter, although your horse may hope there is, especially if he's young or inexperienced. Instead of trying to keep the canter, I train a horse to restart it.

When teaching a horse to become better balanced in canter – and to stay in canter – ride a good working trot around the arena and ask for canter just before the corner. The edge of a school encourages the horse to back off, so he'll start from a canter that isn't too on the shoulder.

Once you're in a good canter, ride a 20m circle and give your horse a bit of rein, so he can use his neck to help him balance; sit quietly and go with him. Before long, the chances are that an unbalanced or lazy horse will try to break into trot. When this happens, ask him to go immediately back into canter – do not spend time rebalancing the trot as a smart horse will latch on to this as a good distraction. The transitions he is making by breaking canter all help his balance, and by having the trot corrected each time, he learns that breaking canter isn't an effective evasion. I find the horse soon decides that the best option is to maintain canter by himself.

CANTER DOS AND DON'TS

- **Do stay on a circle to help you balance.**
- **Don't stick your outside leg back too far to ask for canter, as this encourages hollowing. Instead, use a combination of your outside and inside leg.**
- **Do make half-halts if your horse goes too fast in canter.**
- **Don't take sitting trot before asking for canter, particularly if this is likely to make your horse hollow (see p.10).**
- **Do give and retake the reins (see p.16) in canter from time to time in order to check the horse is in balance. If he is, he'll stay in the same rhythm and outline.**

Ensure your horse is doing a good working trot before you ask for canter

Hiscox Kaluchi is young and still unbalanced in canter at times (top)... but by regulating the rhythm and impulsion he is able to engage and carry his weight on his inside hindleg and balance himself. Here Richard rides Hiscox Kaluchi in a 'light' seat to encourage him to come up through his back

Poles

Poles add a bit of variety to schooling sessions: intelligent horses need plenty to occupy their minds, and poles provide them with something visual to focus on, and they're good for building up a horse's confidence, too. Here are just a few ideas to get you started. A good rule to follow for any exercise you do with your horse is to always begin with the simplest way of doing the exercise, and to finish with the least simple way.

In a line

Set up trot poles approximately 1.5m (4½ft) apart, depending on your horse's stride. I tend to put them on the centre line, because then I can practise my centre lines for tests. Introduce the poles to your horse by riding in between them to start with. Then you can begin to weave your way in and out, keeping your turns large to avoid putting your horse off balance. Once he accepts the poles, move on to trotting through the middle of them. I start with three poles and build up to five poles as the horse gains confidence.

Introduce poles by riding through them first

Poles set out in a fan shape can be used in a variety of ways

Fanning out

If you don't have someone on the ground to help adjust the distances, fanning poles out is a great exercise, because you can shorten and lengthen your horse's stride by riding either the inside or the outside of the fan. If your horse makes a mistake – which he may well do at first – give him plenty of reassurance, so he doesn't lose his confidence. And the next time, you will probably find he sorts himself out!

Lateral work – leg yield

You can do this exercise using just one pole, to introduce your horse to lateral work. Walk a small circle around the pole and then gradually leg yield out on to a bigger circle. Go out a metre at a time until you're on a 20m circle. Kaluchi is crossing well and showing a controlled bend, which will help with his suppleness. This is a good exercise for regaining a horse's attention if he has lost focus.

Clever corners

I've seen people throw away marks in dressage by not riding into corners. So from day one of their training, all my horses learn not to cut corners, and here's how. Firstly, make sure your arena is well harrowed, so that you don't have a deep trench around the perimeter. Walk around the school, and ask your horse to turn as his front legs reach the end of the track. Rather than turning him totally with the inside rein, try to turn your upper body from the waist up. Do not turn the hips and never lose the outside rein contact.

If you make sure you ride into every corner you ever get to with your horse, then cutting them won't be an option he'll consider. Watch how professional dressage riders ride into their corners. Using the whole corner makes the arena feel much bigger, and allows you to prepare for the next movement.

For leg yield, step into your inside stirrup without leaning over – keep your bodyweight central. Nudge the horse over with your inside leg and control the bend with your outside rein and outside leg

Begin the exercise in walk, and ride towards one corner of the arena

As your horse's front legs get close to the track, ask him to turn with your upper body

Hiscox Kaluchi knows cutting corners isn't an option

Counter canter

The best way I have found to introduce a horse to counter canter is to ride shallow (5m) canter loops down one of the long sides of the arena. This is best done in a 60m arena so that the angles of the loops aren't too steep. Try to make your loops gradual, and avoid making abrupt turns.

If your horse stays balanced doing this exercise, then take it a step further. Ride half a 10m circle in canter, returning to the track at not too steep an angle. Stay in counter canter for a few strides on the long side, and then trot. As your horse becomes more balanced, continue in counter canter around the school.

TIPS FOR COUNTER CANTER

- Don't ask for too much bend towards the leading front leg. Keep the neck almost straight with just a very slight bend.
- Ride the exercises equally on both reins.
- Your aids should stay with the leading canter leg, so you will be positioned slightly to the outside of the school, in line with your horse's shoulders, with the leg nearest the arena wall in an inside leg position, and the leg on the inside of the school in an outside leg position. It sounds a bit complicated but if you halt, with you and your horse in a counter canter position, against the track, you'll be able to figure it out easily.

A good test of a balanced horse is to give and retake the reins in counter canter, as Hiscox Chalifas shows here. Does he stay in the same rhythm, balance and outline?

Troubleshooting

As we all know, with horses, things often don't go smoothly. I'm lucky because I get to ride a lot of young horses, which has taught me to anticipate how a horse is likely to think and react. I've demonstrated a few common reactions here.

Spooking

Spooking is a survival tactic for a horse. In fact, a spooky horse is an intelligent horse because he is spooking away from things he sees as potential threats, so therefore he'd probably survive longer in the wild. Young or green horses are more likely to spook from time to time than more experienced ones. After all, they won't have come across as many sights and sounds, so who can blame them?

How you decide to deal with spooky behaviour can make a big difference to how much your horse grows in confidence for the future. The most important thing I've found is not to make an issue of it – beating your horse past a scary object only reinforces his fear of it. On the day of our photo shoot, Kaluchi was particularly worried about the very scary photographer in the corner of the school, and his survival technique kicked in. When I'm confronted with a situation like this, I do my best to ignore the spooking. I turn the horse's head slightly away from the object by lifting my inside hand, then use my inside leg to push him towards the track. By doing this, I'm reassuring the horse that I will protect him, and he'll learn to place more trust in me as our training progresses.

On the next circuit I turn his head slightly away from the camera by lifting my inside hand, then I use my inside leg to push him towards the track

---

RICHARD'S GOLDEN RULES

- Be clear about what you want to achieve with your horse, and above all be realistic. Set yourself smaller goals until you reach the bigger ones.
- Train the horse's mind, not his body, because a horse learns through mental association. An example of this is how all the horses start banging their stable doors when the yard manager arrives in the morning. Why? Because they know they're going to get fed, as the same thing happens at that time every day. Use the same principles when you are training the horse under saddle, by giving the same clear command every time you ask him to do a particular movement.
- Don't bore your horse. My horses do a maximum of four times a week in the school, and with the young ones, I always keep the sessions short.
- Training must never be about what you want, but always what is right for the horse. Under-developed muscles need building slowly, so don't keep on and on if your horse is clearly tired!
- Walk is the explaining pace, so where possible, ride every exercise in walk first. But don't over-collect or you can disturb the four-time rhythm.

Freshness

A fresh horse might not mean any harm, but you could end up on the floor if you're not sensible. If your horse feels fresh, or you know he's prone to the odd buck at the start of a session, put him on the lunge first. If he still wants to misbehave with you on his back, then your best bet is to quietly put him to work. Ride different shapes, and movements such as leg yielding. If you don't give your horse time to think about being naughty, he'll be less likely to misbehave. Keeping him in a good outline will make it difficult for him to buck, and riding him forwards with plenty of impulsion will make him less likely to nap, spook or rear. Always ride fresh horses positively, and keep your horse as much between hand and leg as you can.

Being strong

I often find that sharp horses are quite strong when they first come out. They may be feeling a bit jolly and inattentive, and run away everywhere. If your horse comes into class a bit like this, then keep him on a circle to help with his balance. Move your circle around the school, to add variety. I don't mind my horses having a look at something, but if they try to go against the hand, I am always quick to resist a little with the rein contact until I have them soft again. That's another example of mental association and making ALL your messages to the horse very clear.

- You need to have a very secure upper body position to ride young or unbalanced horses, and the best way to develop upper body strength is to ask someone to lunge you without stirrups on an older, experienced horse.
- Avoid pulling back on the reins to slow a speedy horse. It is fine to give the odd half-halt, but if you get into the habit of pulling back, a) the horse will win anyway, b) the hindlegs will go further out the back door, and c) you'll end up with a horse that's twice as strong as he was at the beginning.

A strong upper body is essential for riding young horses

Cooling down

An important point to remember when you're cooling your horse down is that he is still in the classroom. It's not a chance for him to do as he pleases and run around the arena with his head in the air and his back end strung out behind him. If you allow him to do that, you are being inconsistent, which will not help his schooling. Cooling down is about allowing worked muscles to stretch, and finishing on a calm note, and I do this by riding my horses in the same outline as I do for warming up, so that they lift and stretch their whole topline.

Consider these when you're stretching your horse:

- **Rhythm and balance** Keep the rhythm regular and steady. You can help your horse to balance by staying on a circle during his stretching work.
- **Outline** Aim for your horse to stay in a consistently stretched position, rather than allowing him to drift in and out of the stretch. If he tries to come above the bit, use a little rein resistance, but be quick to be soft with the hands when he returns to his stretch.

- **Ride with some contact** Have the reins at a length where you are still able to influence where the horse is going and what he does. This is somewhere between the contact you'd ride him on normally, and having him on the buckle. Find out where it works best for you and your horse.

Richard always tries to finish on a moment when the horse is beautifully relaxed and calm, like Hiscox Kaluchi is here. In this picture Richard is performing the exercise of 'giving and retaking the reins' to check that Hiscox Kaluchi is not using the reins for support

Leg yield – Carl Hester

This lateral movement is the first you would teach a young horse. It educates him to move off your leg and introduces travelling sideways; it also makes him more rideable because it is a good suppling exercise and improves both turns and corners. Previously a training exercise, leg yield is now required in some Elementary tests.

COMMON PROBLEMS

The steps become shorter
If the horse's strides become short and tight, then you are not allowing enough forward movement, or you are asking for too much sideways movement. Establish a positive, marching walk before trying again, and try to maintain these more active steps – this will be essential for the half-pass (pp.30–31) later in your horse's training.

The horse won't go sideways
If you tense up, your body and weight may be in the wrong place, so the horse won't understand the aids.

Try in a more relaxed situation, perhaps on a hack – just ask for a few steps towards the edge of the track or road. If he won't move over for the correct aids, back up your leg with a touch from a schooling whip; over-using your leg will deaden him to it.

Tilt in the horse's head
In the first photograph (below left) it is clear, because of his white blaze, that Negretto's head has tilted. To correct this, I lift my inside (left) rein to soften his jaw, then I get a truer bend on the outside of his body. And sure enough, his head straightens (below)!

Shoulder falls out
This happens when the rider allows the outside rein to be released, so the horse reaches out too far to the side with that shoulder, instead of maintaining the same angle of forwards and sideways. To correct this, keep the contact on the outside rein, and use it to control the amount of bend in the horse's body.
In the photograph below I have released the outside (right) rein, which allows Negretto's outside shoulder to reach too far sideways.

What happens in leg yield

In leg yield, the horse moves forwards and sideways, with his head and body bent away from the direction of travel. When first teaching it, ride up the three-quarter line of the school and ask for leg yield back to the wall. Most horses hang to the wall, so use this to your advantage! As he moves, keep the horse parallel with the long side of the school, with not too much bend or angle.

Your shoulders and hips should be parallel with the horse's

Open the inside rein to encourage the bend

The outside rein controls the horse's outside shoulder, ensuring that the horse's body remains in an even bend throughout the exercise

Push into the outside stirrup and use your weight to take the horse to the right

Use your inside leg just behind the girth (the more sensitive area) to ask him for sideways steps. Ask with little nudges, rather than one long squeeze

Carl demonstrates leg yield on Negretto, who neatly moves diagonal pairs of legs, matching the reach of the stride each time. Negretto is travelling on the left rein, and leg yielding to the right, so the left leg and rein are the 'inside' aids, and the right leg and rein are 'outside' aids

Shoulder-in – Carl Hester

Shoulder-in is introduced in some tests at Elementary level, but it is also a great exercise for straightening the horse and for making the contact equal on both reins. It encourages the horse to place greater weight on his inside hindleg, which in turn helps to lighten the forehand. Once the hindleg is active, the horse is more supple and manoeuvrable.

Shoulder-in is best ridden at an active trot, and the same rhythm should be maintained throughout the movement. The horse's shoulders are placed on an inside track, leaving the hindlegs on the track. The horse's body is bent around the rider's inside leg, at an angle of about 30 degrees – as a guideline, you should just see the corner of the horse's mouth and eye on the inside.

It is the rider's choice if the horse is on three or four tracks (see box at right), but the key thing is that the same angle is maintained from the start to the finish of the movement.

Shoulder-in step by step

Think of the movement in three parts . . .

1 Ride a 10m circle in the corner of the school before a long side. As you turn the circle towards the long side, keep the horse bent as if you were continuing on your circle, but use more inside leg to ask him to travel along the long side.

2 Maintain the same angle throughout the movement – the wall of the school should help your horse keep the same position. If he stiffens, or you lose the angle, turn on to a 10m circle and start again. Once your horse is established at keeping the same tempo and angle along the wall of the school, introduce shoulder-in movements on the three-quarter line.

3 Finish the movement by straightening your horse before the next corner of the school.

SHOULDER-FORE

Shoulder-fore is not a test movement, but I use it as a training exercise for young horses that find it difficult to stay straight in any pace. Horses often have this difficulty as their hips are wider than their shoulders.

As you ride around a corner in canter, imagine just beginning a shoulder-in movement, but don't make as much of an angle. This will push the quarters back on to the track, and straighten the horse to the outside rein. Try to imagine the horse's inside hindleg landing between the print of his forefeet.

Negretto's inside hindleg can be seen stepping between his forelegs

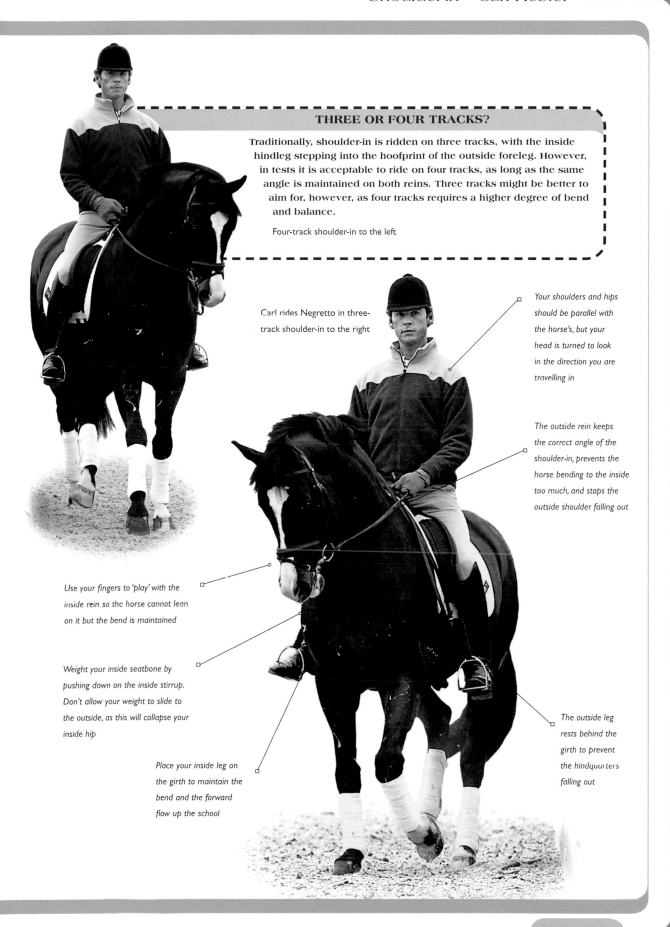

THREE OR FOUR TRACKS?

Traditionally, shoulder-in is ridden on three tracks, with the inside hindleg stepping into the hoofprint of the outside foreleg. However, in tests it is acceptable to ride on four tracks, as long as the same angle is maintained on both reins. Three tracks might be better to aim for, however, as four tracks requires a higher degree of bend and balance.

Four-track shoulder-in to the left

Carl rides Negretto in three-track shoulder-in to the right

Your shoulders and hips should be parallel with the horse's, but your head is turned to look in the direction you are travelling in

The outside rein keeps the correct angle of the shoulder-in, prevents the horse bending to the inside too much, and stops the outside shoulder falling out

Use your fingers to 'play' with the inside rein so the horse cannot lean on it but the bend is maintained

Weight your inside seatbone by pushing down on the inside stirrup. Don't allow your weight to slide to the outside, as this will collapse your inside hip

Place your inside leg on the girth to maintain the bend and the forward flow up the school

The outside leg rests behind the girth to prevent the hindquarters falling out

COMMON PROBLEMS

Quarters into the wall

If the horse's quarters bump into the school wall, this might be because you have not moved his shoulders to the inside track. Ride a circle and allow the shoulders to move off the track (as if still on the circle) before asking the horse to move along the wall. Aim for the outside foreleg to come down on the inside of the track – this will allow the hindlegs to stay on the track.

Too much neck bend

When the rider asks for the shoulder-in with too much inside rein the horse's hindlegs follow the forelegs instead of being on separate tracks, and the horse's head is bent to the inside. This is not true bend! To avoid this happening, use more inside leg to create bend through the horse's body – not just his neck – and use the outside rein to control the angle of the movement.

Shoulder falls out

Probably the most common fault in shoulder-in is the horse falling out through the outside shoulder. It is generally because the rider has used too much inside rein to get the bend and not enough inside leg to support it. Another reason could be that the rider has failed to keep the contact on the outside rein. Ask for less bend until the horse is more balanced on that rein, and keep a constant contact on the outside rein to maintain the same level of bend throughout the movement.

Steps become shorter

If your horse becomes tense, or he does not have enough forward impulsion, his steps will become shorter and choppier. Straighten him, ride forwards boldly, and ask again when the quality of the pace is better. Try riding shoulder-in for short periods only before circling away, to encourage the horse to keep the same tempo, and ride with less angle until he is more established. Don't be afraid to return to leg yielding (pp.20–21), and ride in rising trot to help free his back.

Negretto's neck is bent but his body isn't

Carl and Negretto demonstrate falling out through the outside shoulder

IMPROVE YOUR DRESSAGE MARKS WITH BETTER TRANSITIONS – AMY STOVOLD

Transitions are much more than a means of getting from one pace to another. Riding good transitions helps to maintain your horse's concentration, improve submission, and encourage the horse to step further under his body with his hindlegs and to carry his weight with his hindquarters.

Progressive Transitions

I usually start with progressive transitions, such as medium walk to working trot, working trot to working canter, working canter to working trot, and working trot to medium walk. It's really important that you think about riding forward and uphill into each transition – whether it is an upwards or downwards transition. In the early stages of training, allow your horse to stretch forwards into the rein, but be careful not to let him pull the reins – be prepared to back up the rein aid with your legs if he does.

On a circle

A great exercise for practising trot-canter and canter-trot transitions is to start on a trot circle. Ensure the horse is round and soft in the hand, then ask for a transition to canter halfway around the circle, and then halfway around again, ride a transition to trot. The circle will help you and your horse to remain focused. Once you've ridden this exercise a few times, you should find the trot and canter have improved and the horse works in better balance and accepts the contact. Your aids should become more finely tuned and your horse more responsive.

In this trot-to-canter transition it is clear that riding good transitions encourages the horse to step further under his body with his hindlegs

In a downward transition, it is important to maintain the rhythm and activity in the legs, as here

Travers – Carl Hester

Also known as quarters-in, travers improves the horse's bend and his obedience to the aids, and asks him to engage the hindlegs. The horse moves into the direction of travel, which places more weight on the inside hind as the outside hind crosses in front of it.

Travers is a stepping stone to half-pass. Both are advanced dressage movements, but don't be put off having a go, as they should also be viewed as good training exercises for horses. However, before teaching your horse travers, you should be confident in leg yield and shoulder-in on both reins (see pp.20–21 and 22–24). There is little point in pursuing the next level of lateral work until you have got the basics well established.

COMMON PROBLEMS

Horse's neck too bent

If you try to bend the horse's neck too much to the inside, you may affect his rhythm by suppressing his forward momentum. Bending the neck may also affect the angle of his body so his quarters may not come into the school enough. To correct this, think about the horse's head and eyes looking down the track of the school – looking in a mirror will help with this!

Quarters in too much

Your outside leg asks the quarters to come in on an inside track, but if you ask too much the horse may 'crab' along at too steep an angle. This means that less weight is placed on the inside hind, and it will also affect the horse's rhythm. To correct it, ride a 10m circle and ask again with less outside leg and more inside leg, to create less of an angle so the horse moves forwards freely.

A mirror is useful to check the horse's bend and position

Use your inside leg on the girth to create bend

Making a start

To begin with, it is best to ride travers down the long side of the school, so you can use the wall of the school to your advantage, helping to keep your horse's front legs on the track and the same angle through his body. Start in walk, and progress to trot once you are clear about the aids.

Prepare for the movement by riding a 10m circle in the corner before a long side, so your horse is already bent around your inside leg. Take your outside leg behind the girth and activate the horse into bringing his quarters in, controlling the degree of bend with the outside rein. Your inside leg maintains the forward movement and creates the bend, together with the inside rein.

At the end of the school, ensure you straighten the horse in plenty of time before reaching the corner so all four of his legs are back on the track, otherwise you might teach him to 'crab' around corners!

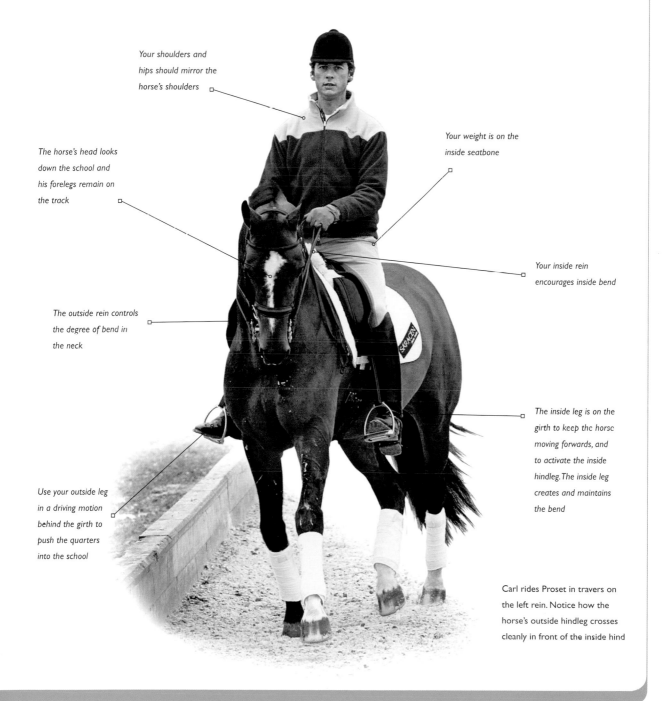

Your shoulders and hips should mirror the horse's shoulders

Your weight is on the inside seatbone

The horse's head looks down the school and his forelegs remain on the track

Your inside rein encourages inside bend

The outside rein controls the degree of bend in the neck

The inside leg is on the girth to keep the horse moving forwards, and to activate the inside hindleg. The inside leg creates and maintains the bend

Use your outside leg in a driving motion behind the girth to push the quarters into the school

Carl rides Proset in travers on the left rein. Notice how the horse's outside hindleg crosses cleanly in front of the inside hind

NINE STEPS TO A CLASSICAL SEAT – PERRY WOOD

Classical riding underpins all modern-day equestrianism, and we can all help our horses to be better and more responsive by using its techniques. The way the rider sits is one of the most important aspects of riding: it's also one of the most talked-about subjects in classical riding. The classical seat is the model for all contemporary types of riding and if you 'sit well' you can influence the horse better, helping him to perform more responsively and beautifully.

The 'correct position'

Students sometimes ask me if they are sitting in 'the correct position', so let's consider if there is such a thing. Riding is a fluid process, and when we are on a horse we need to use our body to feel and adjust what the horse is doing underneath us. Every horse has its own conformation and movement, and humans also have a wide variety of body shapes and sizes. Therefore, in reality, there is no definitive 'correct position' that we all must try to sit in all the time.

So what do we look for in our position? A balanced seat, and a way to sit to help the horse perform the best it can in any moment.

1 Find your balance
Being balanced means being upright, and aligned with the forces of gravity. If you sit in the saddle in a way that works with gravity, rather than against it, gravity will help you stay on board.

To find your true point of balance, experiment by slowly moving your upper body slightly back or slightly forwards, until it's upright. Place your attention on your stomach, lower back and thigh muscles. If you are using these muscles to hold your riding position, you are not in balance. If you are absolutely upright and balanced over your centre, the stomach, back and thigh muscles relax and you may feel slightly as though you are 'floating'. You will also feel 'heavier', much deeper in the saddle and more as though you are sitting 'in' the horse – all without making an effort.

2 Absorb your horse's movement with your seat and waist
A lot of movement comes up through the saddle from the horse's back and into the rider's body, and that movement has to be absorbed by you. If you aren't soft enough, the movement will come out somewhere, like bouncing hands or a nodding head.

When you sit in ways that are in balance and right for the horse, he will immediately start to work better, move with more grace and become lighter in the mouth

To enable your seat to go with the horse's movement, it helps to have 'soft' knees and legs. If they are too fixed, it's difficult to allow your lower body to 'belong to the horse' as it should. More importantly, you may find letting go of them allows the horse to instantly move more freely into a better outline, and be more responsive to the aids.

3 Don't hollow your back...
A hollow back is quite often the result of a rider trying too hard to get a good position. A hollow back is not flexible. The rider's spine must be supple and able to undulate in order to absorb the wave of motion that comes up from the horse's back, especially in the trot and canter. Another result of a hollow back is that the rider tends to sit on the fork of the seat, rather than sitting truly on the softer, central part of the seat.

4 ...or tip backwards
When we first start learning to ride, most of us have a tendency to tip forwards, but then, after we've had a few more lessons, to counteract this fault, we tip a little too far back. Tipping back puts the rider behind the horse's movement and much more out of balance; we're making the horse drag us along with him.

Move slowly back and forward to find the upright position

5 Sit tall – but not too tall!

Because we are told to 'sit up' by our instructor, it can be very easy to overdo things. As with a hollow back, sitting up too much means that the rider's spine and waist is less able to act like a spring and move with the horse. Sitting up too tall can cause people to bounce in the saddle when they are sitting to the trot or canter.

An independent seat comes from having an upright body, soft elbows and shoulders, and loose legs

6 Allow your legs to hang down softly and loosely

By trying to get our legs 'back' and long in what we assume is a correct dressage position, we often end up holding them in place. Instead, allow them to hang softly below the hip. Pushing the legs back means they become tense, which tightens the seat and lifts it away from the saddle. It can also make you sit too much on the crotch. Placing the legs 'back' in a way that doesn't make the rider tighten requires flexibility and looseness in the hip joints, which comes about by practising 'letting go' of the legs over many months.

7 Don't push with your seat

Many riders push actively with the seat wanting more forwardness from the horse or thinking it will help to push the horse's hindquarters more underneath him. An average-sized horse weighs about 500kg, so it's not very likely that a rider 'pushing' will make much difference. Pushing with the seat causes the rider's muscles to tighten, which blocks the horse and may make him hollow away from the discomfort, rather than rounding himself.

8 Sit in the deepest part of the saddle

The deepest part of the saddle is just behind the pommel. This is also the strongest part of the horse's skeleton, where the horse's back 'bounces' the least. It's important to sit here, and to do this sometimes requires a very minute adjustment, which may feel quite strange at first.

We tend to end up in the back of the saddle because we put too much pressure on the stirrups or because we get left behind the horse's movement in trot and canter. Remember to focus on your centre of balance (that means all of you) going forwards with the horse.

9 Let your elbows hang below your shoulders

The classical and centred place for the elbows to hang is below the shoulders. In this position the rider's arms act like soft springs, keeping a consistent contact with the horse's mouth. Arms that are too straight become less 'springy'. If your elbows and hands are too far forwards, you cannot balance without tensing your shoulders; the horse feels this tension in his mouth. There is a temptation to 'give' the hands forwards, but this is unbalancing, putting the horse on his forehand and making us more vulnerable to falling off.

People often talk about riding with 'the seat', and if you have your elbows and hands naturally aligned with your body, the horse will listen to your seat without you having to do anything active.

In a nutshell . . .

The ideal classical seat is balanced in line with gravity, poised, fluid and soft, and moves with the horse. Natural and simple, but not necessarily easy! Try some of these ideas and see how your horse responds, as ultimately, he is your most honest guide.

Check you're riding with loose legs

Half-pass – Carl Hester

Once you and your horse have established travers (pp.26–27) on both reins, you should be able to progress to half-pass without too many problems.

Half-pass follows a diagonal line with the horse moving equally sideways and forwards, bending, and looking in the direction of travel. To start with, ride along the centre line of the school and back to the track in the opposite corner to create a long, shallow angle. As the horse progresses, you can introduce a steeper angle – but only when he is stronger and is confidently going sideways.

Half-pass is a useful exercise for a horse that is very onward bound. It allows you to put your legs on, but to channel his energy sideways as well as forwards, making it harder for him to take control by getting strong and running forwards. It also improves suppleness and, through collection, engages the hindlegs.

Half-pass is introduced in tests at medium level; the angle of the diagonal line is usually shallow to encourage free forward movement. At Grand Prix level the angle is steeper, and sometimes involves zigzagging from left to right and back again in half-pass across the centre line.

Half-pass step by step

1 Bring your outside leg slightly behind the girth, and use it in a tapping, not squeezing, motion to move the horse sideways.

2 Your inside leg on the girth activates the hindleg and works with the inside rein to create bend.

3 Think about pushing weight into your inside heel, as this encourages the horse to step under your weight.

4 The outside rein dictates the level of bend and controls the outside shoulder.

BEFORE YOU TRY CHECK...

- you can ride forwards in trot in an even, active rhythm, in a straight line, and sideways (in shoulder-in and travers);
- your horse is balanced in all paces;
- your horse accepts the contact and can bend on both reins.

COMMON PROBLEMS

The horse doesn't move sideways
You might be sitting to the outside, which doesn't encourage the horse to step into the direction you want to travel in. Weight aids are very important in lateral work, so if you find it difficult to place your weight on your inside seatbone, try looking over your inside shoulder to the horse's inside hindleg, as this will help to position your weight in the right place. Bring your inside shoulder and hip back so you can move with the horse in the direction you are travelling.

TIPS

- Ride lots of travers exercises in preparation for half-pass.
- Start half-pass from a few strides of shoulder-in (pp.22–24) to encourage bend.
- Let the horse's quarters trail a little to maintain the quality of the pace.

- Use your outside leg as an on/off aid, rather than pushing – this is less claustrophobic for the horse.
- Start from the centre line and aim for you and your horse's eyes to be looking at the marker in the opposite corner.

The quarters are leading

This happens when the outside leg is used too strongly before the rider has prepared for the front end to lead – in other words, it is about lack of control or balance. Try riding four half-pass steps and then four steps in a straight line, and repeat, to help re-balance the horse.

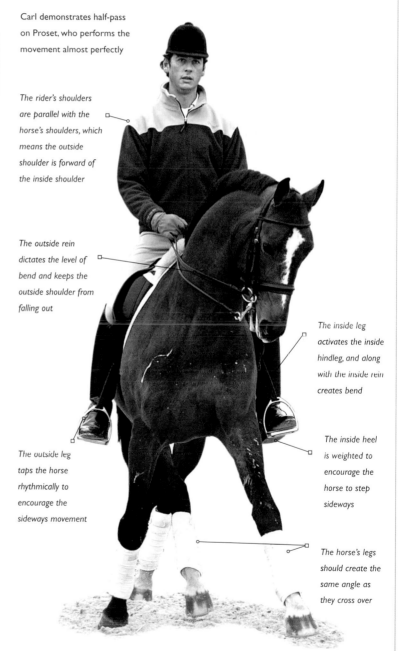

Carl demonstrates half-pass on Proset, who performs the movement almost perfectly

The rider's shoulders are parallel with the horse's shoulders, which means the outside shoulder is forward of the inside shoulder

The outside rein dictates the level of bend and keeps the outside shoulder from falling out

The outside leg taps the horse rhythmically to encourage the sideways movement

The inside leg activates the inside hindleg, and along with the inside rein creates bend

The inside heel is weighted to encourage the horse to step sideways

The horse's legs should create the same angle as they cross over

Renvers – Carl Hester

Renvers is similar to travers (pp.26–27) in that the horse is flexed in the direction of the movement. It differs in that the horse's hindlegs remain on the track, while the forelegs travel on an inner path. In shoulder-in (see pp.22–24) the horse is bent in the opposite direction.

While renvers is not used in competition, it is a good schooling exercise as it teaches the horse to place more weight through the inside hindleg, which helps to develop his suppleness and gymnastic ability. Renvers can also be used to soften the outside rein.

In renvers, the outside aids play a more significant role than they do in travers. This is because the horse does not have the edge of the school to help guide him, so the rider's outside rein and leg must control both the degree and consistency of the bend. For this reason, it is a good training exercise if you have a horse that takes more weight in one rein than the other. If, for example, your horse leans on the right rein, then he will benefit from performing renvers on the left rein, and vice versa.

COMMON PROBLEMS

Too much angle

This occurs when there is insufficient bend in the horse's body. The horse steps sideways, but faces into the school instead of towards the direction in which he is travelling. To correct this, the rider needs to use more inside leg to create more bend, so the horse's head is on a parallel line to the wall. Too much angle can also be caused by the rider sitting on the outside seatbone instead of the inside one. This can happen when renvers is ridden from shoulder-in, as the rider must consciously change their weight aids during the transitions.

Too much bend

Too much bend can cause the outside shoulder to fall out. Ask for only a slight bend to begin with and build up the angle gradually until the horse accepts the outside aids more readily. Only use your inside rein to 'suggest' the bend.

Loss of rhythm/head tilt

If the horse loses his rhythm or tilts his head, it might be because the rider is using the inside rein too strongly, or is crossing it over the horse's neck. Ensure that the inside rein is encouraging bend, but be soft and yielding with it, especially if you are doing this exercise because this is the rein your horse leans on. Be aware of it, and consciously relax the rein.

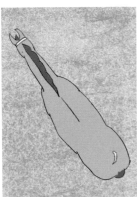

Too much angle

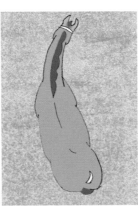

Too much bend

Renvers step by step

The following steps describe how to do renvers on the left rein.

1 Ride correct shoulder-in on the left rein. This gets the horse on the correct angle (about 30 degrees from the track), and it positions the hindlegs correctly.

2 Change the flexion of the horse from the left to the right, by shifting your weight from your left seatbone to your right seatbone, changing your leg position so your right leg is on the girth and your left leg moves just behind the girth. Your left rein becomes the new outside rein, which means your right rein should become looser and lighter as the new inside rein.

3 Now bring the forehand back to the track and ride straight. Maintain the rhythm and impulsion of the pace throughout the exercise. You should find your horse is softer through the right rein.

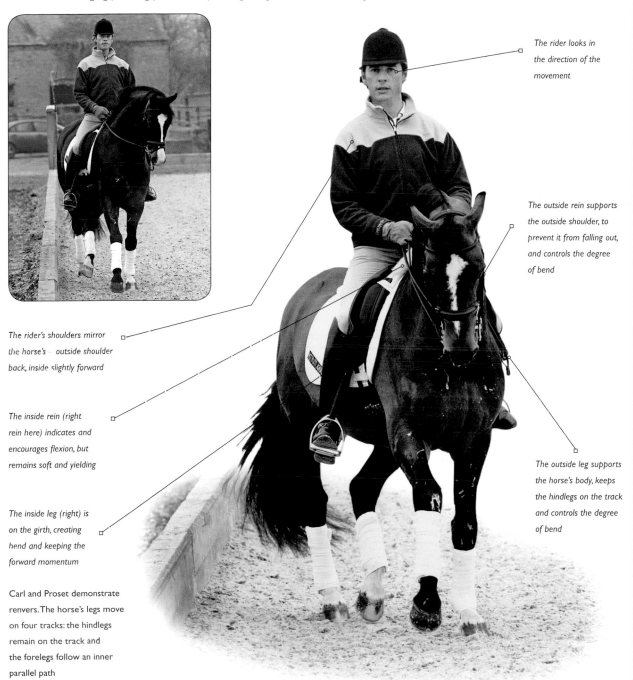

The rider looks in the direction of the movement

The outside rein supports the outside shoulder, to prevent it from falling out, and controls the degree of bend

The rider's shoulders mirror the horse's – outside shoulder back, inside slightly forward

The inside rein (right rein here) indicates and encourages flexion, but remains soft and yielding

The inside leg (right) is on the girth, creating bend and keeping the forward momentum

Carl and Proset demonstrate renvers. The horse's legs move on four tracks: the hindlegs remain on the track and the forelegs follow an inner parallel path

The outside leg supports the horse's body, keeps the hindlegs on the track and controls the degree of bend

THE MASTERCLASSES

While flatwork can be one of the most rewarding aspects of riding, it can also be frustrating and confusing for both horse and rider. When you school your horse on your own it is all too easy to keep slogging away without achieving what you want, and sometimes it can be difficult to know how to change what you are doing to get a better result.

This section consists of a series of lessons given to everyday riders by top trainers. The lessons have been tailored to suit the individual pupil and their horse, but they also focus on common problems to which we can all relate. Each lesson is complete in itself and is intended to inspire as well as educate. If, for example, you have a horse that finds being soft and flexible difficult or one that shoots around the school as if expecting something dreadful to happen, you will find information and practical advice on how to solve the problem and have a successful schooling session. On the other hand, if you have simply been looking for another way to work with your horse, you will also find plenty of ideas here, too.

Flexi-time – Carl Hester

Aim To teach a horse to work equally on both reins using lateral exercises, which will also make him more supple

---

AT THIS MASTERCLASS

Kenny is a 16.1hh gelding that *Sarah* has on loan. 'He has a wonderful temperament and tries really hard. We are currently working at Elementary level in dressage, and my ultimate dream would be to follow in Carl's footsteps and ride at the Olympics one day,' she said.

If you compete in dressage, you'll be aware of how supple your horse needs to be to do well. As you move up the levels, suppleness is even more important as movements get harder. Most horses are stiffer on the left rein, and more supple to the right. If this is so for your horse, when you're on the right rein he'll fall out through his left shoulder, and on the left rein he'll lack inside bend.

Lateral work is not only essential if you want to move up the levels of dressage, but teaching your horse these movements in the course of his training will help to supple and straighten him, too.

Kenny is not unusual in that he is stiffer on his left rein, which means he falls out to the right through his left shoulder

Turn using the outside aids

When a horse is stiff and doesn't want to bend to the inside, the temptation for the rider is to try to bend him by pulling the inside rein. Have a look next time you're at a dressage competition, and you'll see how many riders do this.

I told Sarah to ride a right-rein circle using me as the centre. Always think about turning your horse with your outside aids more than the inside ones, so that on the right rein you bring his left shoulder more over to the right – this is generally the opposite to what he wants to do. Then bring his left shoulder further to the right by closing up the outside rein, so you ride in a shoulder-fore position. Hold this position for about four strides and then straighten up again.

I use this exercise a lot with 'crooked' horses, but it is really important to do some straightforward trot work in between to keep them fresh. Make the whole exercise four strides of shoulder-fore, then straighten the horse up, trot for half a circle, walk and repeat. That way, you keep your horse listening to you and focusing on your aids.

Sarah started to use her outside aids instead of turning Kenny with the inside ones

Lateral exercise 1

I considered Kenny would benefit from some lateral exercises, and the first one I suggested they should try is a simple exercise, which any rider can attempt with their horse, no matter what their level. Ride on to a small circle, say 10m, in walk or trot, and try to keep really straight. Even when you're riding on a circle, both you and your horse need to be straight, which means sitting straight in the saddle with equal weight on both seatbones and equal weight in both reins, with the horse's hindlegs following the tracks left by his forelegs.

Staying straight, ask your horse to move out on to a bigger circle by leg yielding him (see pp.20–21). When you've reached your bigger circle, leg yield back in again to the smaller one.

Watch out for the horse trying to 'escape' by falling out through his shoulder or quarters; use your reins and legs to act as a tunnel, so that your horse always stays within that tunnel. Try not to lose the forward impulsion when you ask your horse to go sideways. Remember that lateral work is both forwards and sideways.

TIME TO THINK

- Spend time on the basics, such as straightness and suppleness, and the harder movements will fall into place later.
- You don't get a supple horse by trotting round and round the outside of the arena, so don't stay in the same pace or movement for too long. Instead, ride lots of turns, circles and transitions to keep your horse's mind and body active.

- Work your horse evenly on both reins, but if he is stiff on one rein, say the left, then think of bringing the left shoulder slightly over to the right to keep him straight, rather than trying to move the quarters.
- Aim to be able to ride your horse with his neck in any position – think Grand Prix test and stretching work! He should learn to stay in the same rhythm and balance, wherever his head is.

Sarah asks Kenny to leg yield on to a larger circle. He responds but is a little resistant

Lateral exercise 2

The next exercise I had in store for Sarah was one that I consider to have many benefits. It helps with the horse's straightness, responsiveness, suppleness, relaxation and engagement – so all in all it's pretty useful!

I asked Sarah to walk across the centre line, ride a quarter pirouette to the left, and then trot away to 'refresh' the horse. At first I helped out with the pirouettes from the ground, by gently tapping Kenny on the hocks to show him where his legs should go. I also told Sarah off for trying to pull Kenny round with the left rein, reminding her yet again that her left hand must be more still. Later she got the idea, and I asked her to

trot away and show me how this exercise had helped. And Kenny had improved: he worked with a more relaxed neck, his hindleg had become more engaged and he rounded his back, making the whole picture look a lot more pleasant and relaxed.

I asked Sarah to stay in working trot on the left rein, and whenever Kenny started to raise and tighten his neck, reminded her that she needed to resist the temptation to lower his head by pulling on the inside rein, but instead, to flex him to the outside a little. She needed to get out of the habit of relying too much on the inside rein; the more you pull it, the stiffer your horse will become on that side.

When trotting away to finish the quarter pirouette exercise, Kenny showed a more relaxed outline

Sarah needs to get out of the habit of pulling on the left rein ...

... so that Kenny 'lets go' more

AIDS FOR A PIROUETTE TO THE LEFT

Shorten the walk, but be sure to maintain the impulsion. The rider's inside (left) rein asks for a little left bend, the outside (right) rein closes against the horse's neck to encourage the forehand to come round, and it also controls the amount of forward movement. The inside leg stays against the girth to help the horse stay bent in the direction of travel, and the outside leg goes slightly behind the girth asking him to step around.

Do some canter work

Think about how you school your own horse at home. Most people do their trot work first and then their canter work, but I believe that's not always the most effective way to get the best from your horse, and explained to Sarah that a lot of horses relax better in trot after they have had a canter. And this was certainly the case with Kenny, because his neck became much more relaxed, and he was swinging more through his back after he had done some canter work. This sort of exercise is all part of the suppling process.

S-t-r-e-t-c-h

The most important part of any schooling session, and the biggest factor in suppling any horse, is stretching. I am a huge fan of stretch work, and am convinced that my horses really do benefit from this training method. I showed Sarah how to get Kenny to stretch well, to really get him working, but in a calm and relaxed way. I explained that carrying her hands lower and wider places the bit on the bars of the horse's mouth, which encourages a lower head carriage. In contrast, a higher hand position encourages a higher head position, probably more suitable for a test situation.

After some cantering, Kenny found it much easier to relax into the trot work

Kenny needs to take more of a contact, but he is starting to get the idea of stretching

CARL'S STRETCHING TIPS

- Your horse will be more likely to want to stretch at the end of a schooling session, so this is the best time to do your stretch work.
- If your horse tries to go too fast, use some small circles to slow him down and rebalance him.
- Your leg plays a big part in getting the horse to stretch. Try to ride him from leg to hand, rather than pulling his head down.
- Use a little outside flexion to encourage stretching.
- A little pat on the neck can encourage your horse to stretch too.

Look sharp, lazybones! – Carl Hester

Aim To improve a horse's response to the leg and get the good work out of him

Lazy horses can be as much of a challenge as sharp ones, and they really make you sweat! They require constant physical and mental effort on the rider's part. I tend to specialize in sharp horses, but plenty of my pupils have stuffy ones, so I had some really useful ideas for Sam and Wally.

Wally is a talented horse, having reached Medium level at the age of 15, just two years after he started dressage. 'He has gorgeous, floaty paces,' Sam told me as she warmed up, 'but he can get very lazy and stuffy. I sometimes feel I may as well carry him around the arena! But we're lucky because he's deceptive, which gets us through tests.'

I promised Sam I wouldn't make the lesson too 'dressagey': you need to wake up a horse like this before you can make a connection!

Effective legs

Sam was making a visible effort to get Wally moving forwards in walk, and I told her not to kick and hold her legs against his sides. I wanted to get her out of big, slow kicks and into quick, sharp ones. At the moment Wally was only reacting when Sam took her leg off, but we wanted him to really go immediately he was asked, and then Sam would be able to get him back.

Carl demonstrates the feeling of 'click and kick', and reiterates to Sam not to keep nagging him with her legs

To sharpen up her leg aids, I asked Sam to try to ride with her legs looser, away from his sides, then to give a sharp 'click and kick'. And when he reacted, to let him go forwards, then pat him, and not hold him back. I told her she wanted him to gallop! I also told Sam to do this repeatedly through the lesson, stressing that if she did it consistently, Wally would eventually react immediately to a light touch of the heel.

As the pair moved into trot, I told Sam we wanted quick strides, not big, heavy ones. And with a horse with a brain like Wally's, it was important not to stay in the same rhythm for too long – one long side would be too much.

I also suggested that changing the rhythm would connect him, so he wasn't so out in his neck, and kept his hindlegs underneath him. You need to keep asking for bigger, then smaller strides down the long side, then make a transition to halt, then 'click and kick', and gallop.

I said it was vital not to squeeze him like he was a tube of toothpaste, but to keep the legs soft, then 'click and kick', and once he was trotting quietly, to keep the legs soft.

I asked for lots of transitions between walk and trot, reminding Sam to keep her legs away from Wally's sides unless she needed to use them. It was important she didn't work harder than Wally, and I had to keep reminding her to walk, 'click' heels, then go, then bring him back again. She needed to be quick and sharp, and to anticipate Wally's anticipation, and not fall into the trap of working harder than him; she needed to recognize it, and get him moving. And when he responded and really wanted to go, I pointed out it would be good for their extended work, too.

A few collected trot strides get Wally sitting back on his hocks (top), and then a quick 'click and kick' from Sam really gets him moving (above)

AN INDEPENDENT SEAT

With the 'click and kick' technique, it's important that you stay secure in the saddle and let the horse go forwards freely – if you give him a jab in the mouth it will have the opposite effect!

You mustn't use your legs and reins to keep yourself in the right position. You need to develop an independent seat.

An independent seat moves with the horse – let your hips swing to take the movement – without affecting your arms or legs.

And how do you get one? Lots of work with a good instructor who encourages you to ride correctly, lunge lessons to deepen your seat, and plenty of hacking that will help develop your ability to react to the unexpected.

A lighter canter

I then asked them to canter, as I planned to use some collection to make Wally 'hotter'. I told Sam to ride a half-halt to shorten him, but warned her not to let him 'die' on her, then to use it firmly again – his comfort zone was to go just a bit faster, but he needed to gallop like he was out hunting!

Wally produced a much lighter and looser canter up the centre line, so I asked Sam to half-pass to the long side and then stay in counter canter. I suggested that when she was training him, not to always ride him like she did in a test, but to let him make a mistake, and then appear like the wicked witch of the west, so that he got a shock if he dropped her.

I then told her to ask him to halt again, to give the rein away, click heels and gallop again; then to go forwards into canter, halt, walk and drop the reins – and by this time he was walking like a racehorse! I reminded her to use a quick sharp leg aid, not to squeeze him, and to give him a pat when he was good.

Sam was working hard, and she commented: 'I've got to be quicker thinking to do this!'

I agreed that she did. Wally is 15 years old, and she needs to find the quickest way to get the movement out of him, because he is really fabulous!

I reiterated that he would shut down if she did lots of long, low work, so suggested she just let him walk for a break, but then picked him up and sharpened him up again. She needs to get him fitter, and to get him out of the school, too. He's lazy, so he needs to do extra things to be fit.

Frequent changes of tempo in canter help to keep Wally's brain working

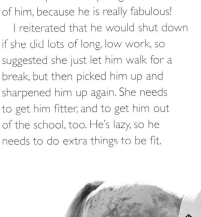

Breaks are kept short with Wally to avoid him 'switching off'

Some tougher transitions

Wally's work wasn't over, and after a brief walk on a loose rein, I asked Sam to get after him again. She was helped by my dog, who suddenly ran in barking!

I reminded her to ride lighter, and then told her to ride walk to canter. She mistimed her first attempt, but on her second, Wally cantered before she kicked him and I was pleased because he went forwards as soon as she took the leg away. That was good – it was a threat he should be worried about!

I instructed her to keep the canter opened up and to turn on to the diagonal, then halt, then legs on and gallop, then take up the reins and canter right. She was doing well and I told her to keep him in that frame – do less! The pair then cantered up the centre line and did half-pass to the long side, with Sam putting the leg on and off to keep the quickness in his pace. Then she had to shorten the canter without holding, then walk. Finally I called to her to canter again – and to take her leg away, and if he didn't respond to the threat, to give him a kick and gallop!

Sam had to really concentrate! I told her to open her right leg, flex him and push him over in canter half-pass. Then to be quiet in counter canter . . . then go on and off with the leg, now make him shorter, collect and step forwards to loosen him, click, and jump him forwards off her leg. I continued to work the pair with lots of transitions between and within the paces, lateral work, changes of direction, and click and kick if the horse got lazy.

I varied the work by asking Sam to do canter travers down the long side, stay in travers and turn up the centre line, then half-pass to the side. Then a half-halt, a transition to walk, then trot, then walk, all designed, as I explained, to get him sharp.

Finishing with a stretch

After several of these exercises, they were producing some lovely work. I told Sam to rise to the trot and let the horse stretch, to move the reins through her fingers, and walk.

Summing up, I told Sam that you really have to use your head with a lazy horse – you always have to be thinking about making him work harder. You have to be mentally quick and strict!

Half-pass in canter, to counter canter, walk, then gallop. I kept Sam and Wally busy!

Spooking solutions – Amy Stovold

Aim To learn to ride without nerves and help a horse overcome spooking issues

---

AT THIS MASTERCLASS

Ashley Rossiter has ridden and owned horses for much of her life. However, a number of bad experiences, including a horse that reared up and fell over backwards on to her, have knocked her confidence.

Otto is a 10-year-old, 16.2hh Warmblood show-jumper. He is a very genuine horse but is a bit spooky, which can frighten Ashley; however, he has never shown any inclination to rear, or displayed negative behaviour. Ashley wants to try showing and dressage with him.

Lost your nerve? Join the club! It happened to Ashley Rossiter, and she found it difficult to overcome her nerves. This was getting in the way of her building a good relationship with her new horse, Otto, and was stopping her from reaching her riding goals.

In my first assessment of Otto and Ashley I observed that Otto has a tendency to be a bit spooky, and that it is his nature to be suspicious of unidentified objects. However, it was important for Ashley to learn how to manage this behaviour, and not reinforce his notion to be scared. While Ashley is a capable enough rider, her nervousness creates a defensive element in her riding, rather than the propensity to establish a mutual trust. This translates to Otto, and it could become an even bigger problem if it is not curtailed.

Otto spots something scary – you can see the tension in his neck – and this fear translates itself to Ashley

Part of the problem

Otto's neck is set on quite high, so when he looks at something, his head carriage becomes even higher! He gets rigid in the neck and backs off Ashley's leg aids. She panics, tips forwards and grips with her lower leg, and also takes a firmer hold on the reins. She tries to rush him past the object, which has the effect of reinforcing Otto's idea that it's a threat. Ashley's reaction to Otto's spooking can be caused by something as small as a glance, or a stop to look at an object, and these can develop into much bigger shies throughout the schooling session.

I started the lesson by helping the pair with some exercises designed to take the worry out of spooky objects, and to help Ashley cope when spooking does occur.

Get the horse listening

I set up some unfamiliar obstacles in the arena, then asked Ashley to ride in. She immediately steered Otto towards the obstacles. I called her back, and told her not to go into an arena ready to pick a fight: this just makes you a defensive rider, and makes your nerves – and your horse's – even worse! I suggested she wait until Otto was concentrating and focused before she approached something spooky.

To get Otto listening, I asked Ashley to warm up on a 20m circle. Ashley was already a little uptight. I told her she needed to learn to breathe, and to relax in the saddle for the transitions to become more fluid. This would encourage Otto to come more in front of and off the leg.

Otto and Ashley practise some transitions until they both relax and start to work better together

---

RELAXED RIDING – TINA SEDERHOLM

Tension prevents riders enjoying themselves and making progress. Most adult riders carry tension in their bodies, and this reduces when they relax. By relaxed, I do not mean 'slumped in front of the television' mode, but in a state of calm attentiveness, because this allows the rider to feel what they and the horse are doing.

- The most common symptom of tension is shallow breathing, or holding your breath completely. If you breathe like this, your stomach doesn't move, and breath gets locked in your upper body, with your shoulders and neck becoming cramped or stiff. If this sounds familiar, take a few deep breaths, letting your stomach expand as you breathe in, and deflate as you breathe out. This releases your shoulders and lowers your heart rate, bringing you to a more relaxed state.

- A rider's tension also often comes out in their hands. If your hands are stiff or tense, try this exercise to help them become more sensitive. Clench your fist around the rein as hard as you can for about 30 seconds. Make sure the rein is loose so you do not affect your horse. Then slowly release the fist so it is still closed, but the muscles and ligaments have softened. Repeat this a couple of times so you start to notice the difference between when your hands are relaxed and when they are tense.

- Another 'trick' that I like to use is to take one hand off the reins and then gently shake it, before doing the same with the other hand. This works especially well when you are sat waiting to go into the competition ring.

Ashley and Otto both look at the obstacle

Riding past the obstacle with Otto's head bent away from it. This is a useful tactic to use when passing a frightening object on a hack, too

Be an effective rider

Despite the fact that he's spooky, Otto is a bit lazy, too, and I observed that he used spooking at the obstacles as an evasion tactic until finally he slowed right down and almost shuffled past them. This sends Ashley into overdrive, and she becomes very animated in an attempt to get Otto past, thus making his spooking even worse!

I then worked on Ashley's position, getting her to sit more on her bottom and to relax her lower leg down. I explained that clamping on with the leg tips the rider forwards, making it easier for the horse to shy any way he wants to. I also helped Ashley to use her legs more effectively. She was nagging the horse with her legs, so I encouraged her to use her legs once, and to back them up with a tap of the whip if Otto did not respond. Soon Otto was moving freely forwards with very little effort on Ashley's part.

This was good, because it showed that now Otto was listening to her, so now Ashley had something left in reserve if she needed more leg to get him past the spook!

Keep focused

With a spooky horse and a rider lacking in confidence, both need to be given plenty to think about in their work to keep their minds focused. I instructed Ashley and Otto to do plenty of transitions from one gait to another, and within the gaits. Although the obstacle was still there, they didn't fixate on it.

I encouraged Ashley to ride gradually nearer and nearer to the obstacles, but with her mind concentrated on something other than the obstacle. An important thing to note is that if the rider is focusing on an obstacle, then so will the horse, perpetuating the original problem!

When they had been past the obstacle a few times, I suggested that Ashley practise riding closer to it but with Otto's head slightly bent away from it. I told her to keep a constant rhythm in her head – no faster and no slower passing the spooky object. Sure enough, Otto had a little look, but he didn't spook. I also encouraged Ashley to pat him, which caused him to lower his head and come into a more relaxed and lower frame, stretching down and out over his topline.

Patting your horse's neck encourages him to lower his head and come into a more relaxed and lower frame

Trust the horse

As Ashley gained confidence, she was able to maintain a good rhythm, to ride past the objects with a more secure seat, and to keep Otto fully focused on her aids. Finally, I asked Ashley to bring Otto down to a walk, lengthen her reins and trust him to walk past the spooky corner, remembering to breathe, relax and trust him. Otto strolled past the spooky corner without the blink of an eye!

I suggested that Ashley had herself videoed riding past several different kinds of obstacle, of the sort that might make Otto spook. This would help her realize how miniscule the spooks in fact were, despite how big they felt to her, and then she could see how well she managed to cope with them. I really do believe that positive visualization is a great way to reinforce to the rider how well they are riding. This, coupled with positive experiences of riding past obstacles without repercussions, will serve to improve both horse and rider confidence levels.

When Ashley trusts Otto, Otto trusts Ashley – there are no spooks at the scary obstacle

---

ASHLEY'S VERDICT . . .

'Today has been fantastic!' Ashley enthused. 'Normally I concentrate on getting Otto going well in my lesson, instead of facing up to my demons, and I have to admit I was really nervous about confronting the spooking. In fact, I had been up since 5am worrying about what we were going to do today!

'I tend to avoid any possible confrontational problems – I stay away from spooky corners, and I don't ride when it's windy. But now I feel much more confident about dealing with Otto's spookiness, and coping with situations during my schooling sessions if they should arise. Amy has shown me how to ride him through it without a problem or it getting any worse.

'Today has gone part of the way to showing me that I can cope with Otto's spookiness. I also didn't realize how much of it was me making the problem worse by over-reacting, and that the less I do, the better Otto is!

'This has been a real learning curve for me, and one which has gone part way to helping me tackle my fear when he backs off my leg and stops to look. I'm feeling really optimistic – it seems Otto and I can respond to good, professional help!'

Lead role – Carl Hester

Aim To teach a horse to canter on the correct lead

It's not at all uncommon for young and inexperienced horses to struggle with canter leads when they first begin their training, but it's something that I'm not usually too concerned about. It's our job as riders to teach the horse, and as long as we are clear with our signals, they'll soon understand what we want. And I explained to Lucy that it's consistency that leads to good results. So whenever you get the wrong canter lead,

immediately come forwards to trot, wait for a good moment, and then clearly ask for canter again. At first you might find that you get twenty wrong strike-offs before you get a correct one, but being consistent will always pay off. At first you should settle for just one or two correct transitions, and then go off and do something quite different and that the horse finds easy, because in this way you keep his confidence.

AT THIS MASTERCLASS

Lucy Stokes has been riding for 15 years. She has owned six-year-old, 16.2hh *Oscar* for two years, and says: 'I find it hard to get right canter with Oscar. In fact, when he does strike off on the right lead, he will immediately change to the left. I've tried placing poles and walk to canter but nothing seems to work. And instructors have ridden him and had the same problem.'

On the left rein, Oscar strikes off on the correct lead every time!

Falling out

I asked Lucy to bring Oscar on to a big circle on the right rein in trot, and suggested she should try to stay as relaxed as possible, because you can't work on a problem if you're tense.

As the pair circled around me in trot, I explained that often when there's a schooling issue, with any horse, it is caused by an underlying problem at a more basic level. And this was undoubtedly the case with Oscar: he was running out to the left because Lucy was letting him 'fall out' to the left, and this was why he was favouring the left lead.

When a horse drifts out like this, you can straighten him by using the outside leg behind the girth to stop the quarters falling out, and closing up the outside rein, creating a 'brick wall' which the horse's left-hand side has to stay within. Oscar's hindquarters were swinging out to the left, which was bringing his head in to the right – he wasn't bending his body in a nice curve! I advised Lucy she needed to do the opposite to what he wanted to do.

I told her to position his head and neck left, so his quarters came right, and then to straighten him up again, and to repeat this every time he drifted until he understood it wasn't correct.

Falling out through the shoulder or the hindquarters is a common problem, which you can see with horses at higher levels as well as at the lower ones. The trouble is, if you ignore it at the lower levels, you'll only find you get more stuck as you attempt the harder movements. The problem becomes even more exaggerated when there is no school fence on the outside to support the horse, such as when you're riding across the school or on an inner track. And that's when your 'wall' needs to be even more effective.

Perfect timing

I explained how important it is to ask for a canter transition at just the right time. I advised Lucy to choose a moment when Oscar felt balanced and wasn't falling out through his quarters – and to ask in the corner rather than on the long side. And just before she asked, to take the horse's head a little to the left, and then give him the signal for canter.

Oscar immediately struck off on the correct lead, so I told Lucy to give him a pat, then trot, and then do it again. I didn't keep the pair in canter for long to start with because I didn't want Oscar to do a flying change. Next time round, Oscar and Lucy got it right again, so I was able to congratulate them both! I suggested that Oscar deserved a break, so told Lucy to ask him to trot, big pats all round, and to walk him for a minute.

AIDS FOR CANTER

First, get a good trot. The inside rein asks for inside bend, and the outside rein stops the horse falling out. Your inside leg stays on the girth, and you ask for canter with the outside leg, behind the girth. Sit up and ask the quarters to step under the horse's body.

Left bend brings Oscar's quarters to the right, and hey presto, he strikes off on the correct canter lead!

Straighten up

As I said earlier, many problems will start to improve once the horse is straighter. And if, like Oscar, your horse is stiffer one way than the other, work on his straightness on both reins, so you school him evenly. So for example Oscar, who falls out badly on the right rein, will have a tendency to fall in on the left rein. To help with this, on the left rein Lucy needs to keep a firm outside rein contact (right rein), step into her inside leg so she can use it to keep Oscar out on the circle, and use an open inside (left) rein to help with inside bend and prevent him falling in through the inside shoulder. This all helps to create a straighter horse, which will ultimately help in getting correct canter leads.

Oscar tends to fall in on the left rein

GETTING THE CORRECT CANTER LEAD – OLIVER TOWNEND

There are various ways to ask a horse for the correct canter lead, but I'm quite old-fashioned. I put my outside leg behind the girth, and my inside leg on the girth, and squeeze. I keep the contact on the rein dead even, as it was in trot. And I keep my body still. It's very easy to collapse your body and let the horse run on when you're first training him, so it's important to keep your body strong and still and upright.

Oliver Townend on Flint Curtis

Lucy brought Oscar back on to a right circle to do more canter transitions, and this time he gave a wrong strike-off. I explained that the reason for this was that at the last minute Lucy had let him take his quarters left. I suggested she try riding down the long side keeping his quarters right and his forehand on the track; I told her to stay in this position until she reached the corner, and then to ask for canter. I congratulated them as they got it right. Then I told Lucy to circle Oscar in canter to make the canter more balanced, so he knew he had done as she asked. In fact his canter wasn't bad when Lucy kept his quarters in line, it was just the transition that was the problem.

Once Oscar had cantered a full circle, Lucy went back to some easy exercises, on my request. You should never ignore the tough stuff, but do easier bits in between, so the horse stays confident and so you don't over-stress joints and muscles.

Lucy was worried about positioning Oscar in left bend before a canter transition in a test situation, but I reassured her that it was better to do that than get the wrong lead. Okay, so you might get a comment from the judge about your

Not so perfect. Lucy lost control of Oscar's outside shoulder at the last minute. The result? A wrong canter lead

Lucy rides down the long side in trot keeping Oscar's quarters right and his forehand on the track

Leg yield can help you obtain the correct canter lead, though Oscar is resisting a little here

lack of bend, but you'll be more heavily penalized for a wrong strike-off! And it would only be a short-term thing anyway, just until Oscar understood what Lucy wanted him to do – which wouldn't take long if she was consistent with her training.

I told Lucy another way to get the correct canter lead. You go on to the left rein in trot and turn up the three-quarter line, then leg yield back to the track, aiming to reach it at the corner. Leg yield into the corner and ask for canter as you reach it.

The reason I asked Lucy to leg yield from left to right is to position Oscar's head left and his quarters right – the opposite to what he wants to do, which will help to straighten him up! Oscar was a little reluctant to cross his legs over in the leg yield (see left), but even so, I reminded her to be careful not to draw her leg too far back: better to keep your left heel down and nudge the horse across. If he doesn't listen, give him a tap with the whip. (For more information on leg yield, see pp.20–21.)

A FEW FINER POINTS

- When you ask for the canter transition, make sure your aids are strong so that your horse is clear about what you want. You can fine-tune later when he understands what you want.
- Keep your fingers closed around the reins so that you have a contact with his mouth.
- Don't start to build the canter transition into a big thing. Try to relax and sit quietly. And don't tip your body forwards!
- When he gives you a correct strike-off, give him a pat on the neck so he knows it's right.

Instant improvement – Nicky Barrett

Aim To make small changes in your approach to training to get more out of a horse

I made my assessment of the pair as they rode around to warm up. My initial thoughts were that Joey had three good, active paces but that he needed to be softer through his back, so I showed Lucy a simple exercise in walk, which I thought would really help him with this.

I told her to keep a contact, but to allow him to take the rein forwards and down, making sure he kept the arch in his neck. When you do this it is important to let the horse get his nose forwards, so he's stretching his whole topline and rounding his back, and allow your hands to follow through as he uses his neck. If your hands are too still, you'll stilt the walk. Don't set against him with your upper body, but go with him.

Pay attention to his rhythm in the walk (that is, make sure it's an even one-two-three-four), and keep him in front of the leg so he is going forwards but not hurrying.

AT THIS MASTERCLASS

Lucy Faulkner and her horse *Joey Sorrento*, a 13-year-old Appaloosa gelding, are working at Elementary level in dressage. They have the flying change fairly well established, and have started learning half-pass and walk pirouette. Joey has had a lot of success in eventing, show-jumping, showing and, most recently, dressage. At the time of Lucy's lesson, he had 90 dressage points – when a horse gains 149 points, it moves up to Medium level. Lucy would particularly like help with their left lateral work. 'Joey can get a bit tense and then he loses his forward momentum,' she says.

A good warm-up

I told Lucy to go forwards to trot and do the same thing. I explained that warming up the horse in a deep outline gently stretches and warms up the muscles, plus it helps the horse to relax. But I warned her not to go too fast, as this would encourage the horse on to the forehand.

To finish the warm-up I told Lucy to loosen Joey up in canter. His canter needed more activity, and I instructed her to be loose in her body, to follow the movement of the canter with her seat – you mustn't tense up – and to push her hips forwards, too. In left canter, Joey lacked inside bend and put in the occasional flying change. I explained this was happening because Lucy wasn't stepping into her left (inside) stirrup enough. Her left leg kept coming back, so technically, she was asking him to change – he was doing what he thought she wanted him to do!

Joey needs more activity in his canter, and Lucy needs to push her hips forwards and follow the movement of the canter more

Joey takes the rein forwards and down and stretches his whole topline. It is a nice picture although ideally his nose would be further forward

A purposeful trot

It soon became clear that Joey's trot wasn't active enough, and when Lucy pushed him on, he just went faster and trailed his hindquarters – he wasn't tracking up.

I had a few suggestions to help activate Joey's trot. First I asked Lucy to alternate between sitting and rising trot, changing every few strides, as rising gets better forward movement, and sitting helps to keep the hindquarters engaged. When doing this, when you rise, shorten the distance from your hips to your hands to help with roundness and engagement, and when you sit, allow your hands out in front of you more, so the horse doesn't start to 'stuff up'.

In sitting trot, make sure you sit tall, and that you have a light seat. Keep your inside leg on the girth and use it when you need more impulsion. Keep weight in your elbows, not in the hand, in order to have a soft forearm so you're not tensing up against the contact.

I also had to remind Lucy to ride inside leg to outside rein, particularly on the left rein, when she is inclined not to step down into her left stirrup enough, which makes Joey look to the outside. Finally I asked her to relax the inside hand contact, explaining that if you're pulling back on the inside rein, your horse will feel trapped.

Joey isn't tracking up in trot

Rising trot helps to get better forward activity, as Lucy and Joey demonstrate

Better corners

I then moved on to discussing how to ride corners properly. Many dressage riders lose marks because they don't plan ahead. For instance, if the test asks you to trot down a long side and circle at A, then use the long side to plan the circle. And don't forget that circles have four points!

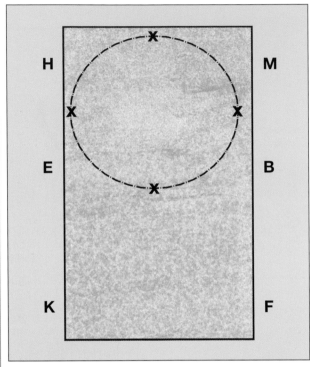

Circles are round and have four points

Ride good corners and the movements that follow will be better

I explained how riding a good corner can gain extra marks. Horses generally try to slow down through corners because it is more effort for them, so you should be aware of this, and ask for more power on the approach to a corner. I also pointed out to Lucy that several movements, such as medium trot and lateral steps, often happen after a corner, and if your corner lacks impulsion, the movement that follows will suffer too.

> **CIRCLE TRICK**
>
> When you're riding a circle, keep the horse straighter by closing up the outside aids – that is, your outside rein and outside leg – otherwise the horse will 'fall out'.

Sideways action

Lucy's main concern about Joey was that he 'stuffed up' when she asked him to go sideways. She felt he lost all his forward momentum, particularly in travers to the left.

I said I thought perhaps Joey didn't understand what she was asking, so suggested she ask someone knowledgeable to push his quarters over, to make it clearer to him. In this movement, you need to use your left leg to keep forward momentum, and if the horse stops going forwards, give him a quick reminder. At first it is best to ride only a few steps of travers, then ride straight again to keep him thinking forwards.

Finally I suggested Lucy start travers in walk, and when she progressed to trot, if Joey did get stuffy, to go rising trot to get the movement more forwards, then take sitting trot again.

After I had watched the pair perform travers and shoulder-in, I had a few more comments to make. I suggested that on the left-rein shoulder-in, Lucy needed to step down into her left stirrup more, and explained that in her efforts to take her weight to the left, she was actually pushing her body out to the right. I then asked her to take her right stirrup away, to stop her pushing down to the right, and then to step down into her left seatbone and left stirrup more.

I had a few more ideas to help Lucy's lateral work. Because she tended to have more weight to the right, I suggested she practise lateral work without her right stirrup, and step down into her left leg and left seatbone, keeping her weight left, too. You should keep your own shoulders in line with your horse's shoulders, because when a horse stuffs up it's because his rider is blocking him. Ask yourself whether you could be hindering your horse in any way, and sit in the same direction as you want him to go in the two-track work.

Nicky helps Joey understand what is required of him in travers

At times Lucy was inclined to ride Joey with too much inside bend. I explained that she was pulling too much on the inside rein, and suggested that if she kept the horse's neck straighter and took more of a contact on the outside rein, not only would she have a better amount of inside bend, but the contact on the outside rein would help to keep him rounder, too. Also, when you do this, if you shorten your reins up a bit more, then you can carry your hands more out in front of you and make any minor adjustments subtly, without pulling back.

The horse should flex from the jowl but stay straight in the head and neck. I told Lucy that at the moment, Joey's bend was from the withers, which was causing him to fall out through his outside shoulder and go on the forehand. Lucy took more of a contact on the outside rein and then carried her hands out in front of her more, and this corrected the problem straightaway.

Lucy's weight has gone over to the right in the shoulder-in, when it should be more to the inside

Lucy takes more of a contact with the outside rein and holds her hands out in front more, which gets Joey off the forehand

Straight canter

Lucy was also concerned about the quality of Joey's canter, and told me that 'In medium canter in particular he swings his quarters in.'

I replied that this was a common problem. You can ask anyone who judges dressage frequently and they'll tell you they see this a lot. The majority of horses are stiffer on one side of their body, and crookedness is more likely to show up in the medium and extended work.

To help this problem I always suggest trying the following:

• Firstly, don't try and correct it by overbending the horse to the inside.

• As you come on to the long side, put the horse in a shoulder-fore position and collect the canter up before you start the medium canter.

• Keep your weight down into your left stirrup and keep a contact on the outside rein, so that he can't fall out through his shoulder.

• Sit down in the saddle, push your hips forwards, and keep the hindquarters active.

• If the horse won't give you a medium canter he's blocked somewhere, so unblock him – in other words, check that *you* are not the cause of the problem.

Ending on a good note

To finish the session, I wanted to see Joey in a good, loose, swinging trot. The canter work had loosened him up tremendously, and he was much more in front of Lucy now. I reminded her to alternate between sitting and rising trot to keep it that way, and to keep her weight into her inside seatbone and stirrup. I know I kept nagging at poor Lucy, but I just wanted to check it had all sunk in!

If you asked me for my opinion, I'd say Joey's a real fun horse. When you ride him in the right way he goes correctly, and when you ride him wrong he stops working so well for you. I consider Lucy will learn a lot from this horse.

Compare Joey's back in this trot with his way of going during an early canter (right): you can see he has loosened up, and is doing a lovely swinging trot

LUCY'S VERDICT

'As we were finishing off the lesson, Joey felt amazing. He was suddenly going forwards properly and felt much more powerful than before. I often get comments in my tests saying he needs to be more forwards, so it will be interesting to see what they say next time, if I can ride him more like this. I thoroughly enjoyed my lesson, so thank you, Nicky!'

When Joey begins the lesson it is clear he needs to be softer through his back

Making connections – Richard Davison

Aim To connect a horse through his body so that he can use it more athletically

---

AT THIS MASTERCLASS

Frances Turner is a keen dressage rider who rides most evenings. *Syeman V* is 17.3hh, a 6-year-old Dutch gelding and a son of Monaco, by Animo. Frances has high hopes for Syeman, whom she bought after selling her two previous horses. He was imported in 2004 from Holland, where he had show jumped. Having qualified for the semi-finals of the Winter Dressage Championships at Novice level, he was due to tackle his first Elementary test soon after this masterclass.

I explain to Frances that Syeman's neck muscles are preventing him from connecting through his whole body, and that he needs to free up these muscles more by working with a lower neck

Frances told me that she'd had Syeman for eight months since she bought him from her trainer, Julie Rowbotham, and they had spent that time getting to know one another. 'My biggest problems are that he is inattentive, and he can become very strong,' she confessed, 'although I do find that the more he goes out, the better he gets.'

I reassured her that that would always be the case with a youngster, but told her not to worry, and just to ignore it for the moment. I asked her to work him in for 10 minutes, as she would at home.

Assessment

After a few circuits, I told Frances to try a canter – at which point Syeman spooked and ran off! I said not to worry; horses often spook at the banners, and he would soon settle.

Watching intently as Frances walked, trotted and cantered on both reins, my first impression was, what a nice horse we had here! You could see he had three good paces, he was nicely put together, and was naturally uphill – in fact, he had loads of good points. His way of going just needed 'tweaking' a bit, to make the best of him.

My conclusion from this assessement was that Syeman was not really 'connected' – he carried his neck far too high, his back was tight, and he wasn't stepping through with his hindlegs – but I had some good ideas to help improve these things!

From neck to hindleg

I began by talking about Syeman's neck and back, and how the two are connected. I explained that at times, his hindlegs were slow and out behind him, but that was because his back muscles were tight, rather than him not being able to step through. To free those muscles up, you need to get the horse's neck lower, and to do that you need to teach him to give in his neck muscles to a passive contact.

I called Frances over and asked her to halt Syeman beside me; I picked up the rein myself, and showed her how to use a passive contact. You use your finger to tighten up the rein until the horse gives. With a passive hand you can increase the tension, and then decrease it as he makes it more comfortable for himself by relaxing his neck muscles. Every time he comes against the bit it will feel uncomfortable for him, then as his head comes down it will feel more comfortable. It is incredibly important that he learns how to yield to this contact.

I sent Frances back out in walk, with the instruction to be very careful to keep her thumbs uppermost. As the horse collects, he will bring his shoulders up naturally. Then you have

Syeman has a tendency to be a bit slow with the hindlegs

When a horse collects, his shoulders will come up naturally

to be very flexible with your wrists and elbows, and ask for medium walk – make him take the contact, instead of dropping it; then you collect him and activate the walk. This exercise helped Syeman to be good in his neck – just what we wanted!

I told Frances to stop and give Syeman a pat, and then to do the exercise again, activating the walk and the hindleg almost to the point of piaffe. This went well, so I asked her to do the same in trot. She repeated the exercise, and as she did so I advised her that if the horse doesn't respond the first time, to give him a little kick as a reminder.

Frances changed the rein and repeated the exercise to the left. Syeman resisted the contact, and I reminded her that if he stiffened against the bit, then she was to make it uncomfortable for him by taking a stronger contact, so that he chose the more comfortable option of his own volition!

Working towards half-halt

I instructed her to bring the circle in, then leg yield out of it and ask for walk. As Frances attempted this exercise, I had to warn her not to let him fall flat on his face! It had taken them about half the circle to get a decent walk, which was too long.

Frances repeated the exercise, and I observed that that time they took quarter of the circle – so you could tell the horse was learning. On the fourth repetition it took just two steps – Syeman was obviously realizing how to make it nice for himself; I asked Frances to repeat it once more.

As Syeman was doing this exercise so well, I told Frances to repeat it again, circling in trot, leg yielding out and then almost walking, but just keeping him in trot, increasing the difficulty and teaching him the beginnings of the half-halt.

ACTIVATE THE BRAIN

During the lesson, I reminded Frances that activity doesn't start in the hindlegs, it starts with a signal in the brain – the spark plug. Take that out, and the best engine in the world is useless. Every bit of training starts in the horse's mind. I can show you any number of impressive horses who have all the talent, but mentally don't want to do it, and because of that, they will never really be any good. You can generally 'make' a horse do something, but he won't necessarily like it, so you have to give him the choice that the right way is comfortable and the wrong way is not. If he comes up with the right choice, he will like it and we can use this to our advantage.

The perfect example is if a horse turns his head. We don't stop him, we just make it less comfortable for him by taking up the contact on the opposite rein so the most comfortable way for him to proceed is to stay facing forwards.

Frances set to work. I told her to make sure she kept up the activity – you should always think of climbing a staircase in terms of your goals with your horse, so you are always pushing the boundaries with what you ask. They did the exercise well, so I called her over for a chat, and to give Syeman a break.

Leg yield on a circle asks Syeman to work through his body more and he begins to connect up

Syeman starts to understand what is needed, and offers us some really nice trot work

Connecting up the horse

As Syeman had a rest I told Frances there was a big difference between a horse taking his neck down and stretching, which is what we did earlier, and connecting – they're worlds apart. So now I wanted to send Syeman out, and help him start to connect. I explained we would do this in stages. Each time you ask a horse, he'll find it harder, but he has to learn to stretch his back muscles. A rule of thumb, to check whether your horse is coming through, is this: if, when you ask for more, he doesn't retaliate in some minor way, you are getting there.

Frances picked up the reins again and took Syeman back out on a circle. After a couple of circuits I was able to tell her his neck was now brilliant, which meant his back was good, and I told her to keep asking for that little bit more. For this you must be sure your wrists stay supple, just as you want the horse's jaw and poll to be. Occasionally flex him to the outside to relax his neck, and try sitting trot – it shouldn't feel any different. Syeman looked great – there were sparks coming off his hocks – and I called out, 'Just look at that trot, that came through connection!'

At this point, one of my dogs rushed in, which made Syeman fire up. I told Frances to quickly use that extra engagement for a last bit of trot, which he did beautifully – then to walk and give him a long rein. As she walked Syeman around to cool off, my one last piece of advice was always to keep raising your expectations, but without upsetting your horse's confidence. And if you feel you are pressuring him too much, just back off and start again.

After all his hard work, Syeman was allowed to walk on a long rein to finish on a relaxed note

Soft and supple – Christopher Bartle

Aim To teach a horse to bend, achieve better balance and accept the aids

I have taught Liz and Archie before, so I know their strengths and weaknesses. This horse is a nice sort with good paces, but there are three basic things that we need to work on at this stage of his career: lateral bend, balance, and the acceptance of the bridle and aids.

I asked Liz to warm up on the right rein, and the first thing I noticed was Archie's lack of inside bend, particularly around corners. I told Liz that to improve your flatwork, you need a horse that is willing to show good inside bend on both reins. I often see riders asking for inside bend by opening the inside rein, but then they forget to allow with the outside rein, so the horse is unable to bend through his neck.

Achieving bend

After my assessment, I offered Liz a plan of action. I suggested that as she approached a corner of the school, she keep Archie's attention to the inside – in this case, to the right. For this, you should make sure your inside rein is short – position your inside hand at the wither to avoid it sliding forwards. Step into your inside stirrup and use your inside leg to push the horse into the corner. Remember to allow with your outside rein – in fact, pat him on the left-hand side of his neck to encourage him to relax and accept your request.

I added that suppling up a stiff horse is a bit like softening a piece of metal – you have to bend it both ways to make it softer. But every horse is different, and some horses are too 'rubbery' through their bodies, in which case you would lessen the amount of inside bend – basically, to improve a horse's way of going, you usually need to do the opposite to what the horse wants to do, though be careful not to overdo it.

Archie tends to cut corners so he doesn't have to bend, because for him, bending is harder work and requires good balance

---

AT THIS MASTERCLASS

Liz Edge shares her horse *Archie (Turkish Delight)*, a seven-year-old Irish-bred gelding, with her partner, Gary Hulland. Liz describes herself as being quite a novice rider, and as her horse is fairly novice, too, they are learning together. Liz enjoys hacking, but would also like to do some dressage competitions.

Liz says Archie is quite spooky. 'He's scared of everything! He needs to gain confidence and have better acceptance of the contact, plus he needs to find his balance and improve his canter.'

When Liz tries giving with the outside rein and stepping into the inside stirrup she pushes Archie into making a better bend on the next corner

Achieving calmness

Like a lot of young or green horses, Archie tends to charge off if he gets confused or if he is scared of something. In fact I don't have a problem with inexperienced horses being like this because it means that the horse is what I call a 'reactor'. Archie might react to things by spooking or running away, but it still means he is reacting, so all we need to do is discover how to channel the energy in the right way.

I explained to Liz that you can achieve calmness through discipline. If you are consistent with your training and always ask the same questions, and are clear about what you do and don't want from your horse, then his confidence will build up and you should soon have a willing and obedient horse. Problems occur when riders get a bit lazy (we've all done it), and on one day out of three allow the horse to perform a poor corner, or charge off without correcting it. The horse then gets confused about what is required, and when the rider decides the next day that she wants better inside bend, the horse questions it! Being disciplined with yourself will get you quicker and better results, and give you a happier horse, too!

I show Liz how to fix her hand at the wither to stop her reins slipping

STRAIGHTNESS – PETER STORR

How does a horse evade going straight?
Quite often, the horse will bring his quarters in, and this is caused by the rider not keeping the horse into the outside rein, and bending him too much to the inside. If you lose the horse's outside shoulder, the quarters come in.
How can you straighten up a crooked horse?
If you lose the horse through the outside shoulder, take a bit of outside flexion, using the outside rein as an indirect rein, i.e. bringing it against the neck.
How do you know when your horse is straight?
Look down at the front of the saddle and imagine a line running through the gullet of the saddle and following the horse's neck. Check that your line follows a straight line or an even curve when you're riding on a circle, and that it doesn't break anywhere.

So when Archie spooked or charged on to the forehand, I had the following advice for Liz:

- Keep a short contact on the reins, and place your hands at the withers so the reins don't slip through your fingers.
- Ride with a strong back. Remember, the horse's neck is stronger than our arms, so the more upright we can stay, the more chance we have of keeping control.
- Stick to your guns and wait, and if the horse doesn't start to rebalance himself, then make a downward transition to walk until he is calm again.

Correct contact through leg yield

Archie was being quite resistant in accepting a good contact, and as his balance and rhythm often changed, it was difficult for Liz to be consistent. I asked if I could have a ride, to see what was happening – I told Liz I wanted to try to free him up a bit in his neck and back.

Once on board, I found that Archie was setting his muscles against me, when actually I wanted him to do the opposite. I found that if I changed from one rein to the other, Archie 'blocked' and, as I explained to Liz, was then reluctant to change his inside bend.

I showed Liz something to try when this happens: if you lift your inside hand up towards the horse's outside ear (without crossing it over the neck), it puts the bit into the top corner of the mouth and encourages the horse to bend to the inside; it also lifts his inside shoulder so that he can't fall on to it. I explained to Liz that I wanted to be able to take Archie wherever *I* wanted to go in the school, rather than feeling that he was wandering in whatever direction *he* wanted to go.

As Archie was falling on to the inside shoulder and ignoring my inside leg aids, I asked him for some leg-yield steps (see pp.20–21) so as to make him lighter on the inside rein and to stop him falling on to his shoulder. If the horse doesn't listen to the leg, then you can use the back of your lower leg and ask more firmly.

It was Liz's turn again, and I asked her to ride a small circle, using me as the centre point, and then to leg yield out on to a bigger circle. I wanted her to get the feeling of Archie being light in her inside hand and with better inside bend, and suggested that when she had leg yielded on to the bigger circle, to do a full circle and then come back on to a small circle, so he didn't lean on her again.

On the small circle, I insisted that Liz tried to keep an upright posture. Each time that she looked as if she was going to tip forwards I told her to think 'Up, up with your body!'. It is really important that you have a strong upper body, and is something that anyone can practise a lot at home. But being nagged by me worked, and Liz very soon stayed taller in her position, and as a result Archie was then in much better balance and control.

Liz has a tendency to tip forwards (inset), but I soon had her sitting up taller (main)

Leg-yield steps help to make Archie lighter on the inside rein

By the end of the lesson, Liz and Archie were working really well together

CANTER QUALMS

Archie's canter is his weakest pace, and Liz struggles to maintain it; however, I suggested she'd find it easier to maintain canter when her position was stronger. Anyone who has trouble keeping their horse in canter should not neglect the issue. You can practise cantering in straight lines out hacking, where it is easier for the horse, starting with short bursts, and then gradually building it up.

Balancing act – Christopher Bartle

Aim To continue a horse's training towards self-carriage

Immi is a sharp mare who doesn't like to hang around, but I believe that's a good quality for any competition horse to have. I have a saying that the hardest horse to train is a statue – I'd much rather train what I call a 'reactor', like Immi – and even if the horse is too sharp when you start your training, this type of horse will always have an engine, so with time and patience you will get there. With a lazy horse, you tend to run out of steam after a while.

Having a reactor is particularly important if you want to event, from a safety point of view as much as anything, because for cross-country you really need a horse that wants to go.

AT THIS MASTERCLASS

A few years ago *Emma Brazier* had a nasty fall while eventing, which left her with a number of injuries. As a result, she has put a hold on her eventing career and is currently doing dressage.

Imprimis (Immi) is a very green six-year-old mare by Master Imp. Emma is currently bringing her on to sell, and thinks she will make a great junior event horse.

GETTING RID OF THE PULL

As Immi is still quite green, she has a tendency to run on to the forehand, so I showed Emma a way of holding her reins to stop Immi pulling and Emma bracing against her. You hold both reins in your outside hand and just the inside rein in your inside hand – this is what I call a single bridge, and its benefits are as follows:

- Your outside rein can act as a brake whenever you want it to, and to apply the brake you simply brace your hand into the horse's neck.
- Your inside hand can slide up and down the rein, depending on the amount of bend you want.
- If your horse spooks suddenly, you are able to move both hands as a pair, rather than pulling on one rein, which might upset the horse further.
- Holding the reins in a single bridge gives you a more secure position, which is a great confidence giver.
- With the reins bridged, the rider can't be tempted to pull against the horse all the time, and will therefore ride the horse on a lighter contact.

I show Emma how to bridge her reins, which should give her more control

Balance through transitions

I told Emma to ride around the outside of the arena, as this is when Immi is likely to bowl on. I advised her to stay in working trot with her reins in a single bridge, reminding her that when the horse bears down on the rein or runs on, to sit up, half-halt with your outside rein (your brake) and be light again.

Remember, a horse isn't born with an instruction manual, so it's our job, as riders, to explain clearly what we want. Immi needs to accept a light contact and work in better balance – that is, take more weight on to her hindlegs and lighten the forehand. She also tends to overbend, which I call 'rolling over'. I advised Emma that when the mare did this, she should sit taller, lift her hands slightly to raise the poll, and then be light again.

Emma found she was having to make lots of half-halts to keep rebalancing Immi, but I told her that was fine. As long as you keep correcting the horse, they'll start to learn what you want – though be careful not to start jabbing the reins.

Next I wanted Emma to make some transitions. I told her to pick a marker and ask for a transition to walk at that marker. In this exercise, when the horse takes its first walk step, soften your hand until it's light, and then trot again. Try to get to the stage where you can lighten the contact before the transition happens, to teach the horse to be soft in its transitions. This exercise also helps with balance and control.

HOW TO HALF-HALT

To half-halt, sit tall and think of making a downward transition. Take a little feel by increasing the pressure on the outside rein. As your horse slows, ask him on again. This shifts his weight more to the hindquarters.

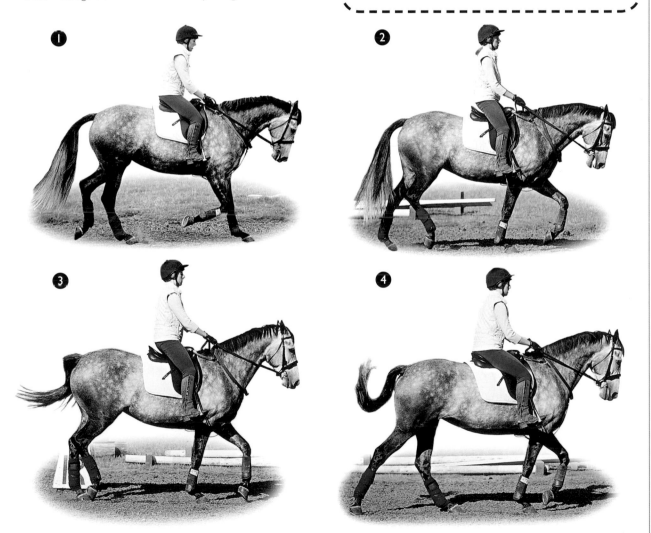

When Immi became strong in the hand…Emma sat tall and asked for a walk transition. Immi hollowed her outline a little but then became soft in the hand again

A well balanced horse will stay in the pace it's in – and go from one pace to another – with a light rein contact. A good test is to give the rein away for a few strides (see p.16), to see if your horse stays in the same rhythm and outline – he shouldn't rush off or lose balance.

Riding single-handedly

I had a new challenge for Emma: to make it her goal to ride a 20m circle with both reins in the outside hand, but with her inside rein short enough to allow her to turn. In this exercise, when you want to turn, keep your weight into your inside stirrup and turn your body the way you want to go. Every now and then, pat the horse on the neck with the inside hand so that he stays nice and relaxed.

I stood in the middle of the school while Emma rode Immi in a circle around me with one hand on the reins. I suggested she think of driving a car. Before you turn a car, you need to slow down, so just before each touching point of the circle (at 3, 6, 9 and 12 o'clock, see diagram), make a half-halt to slow down and then make your turn.

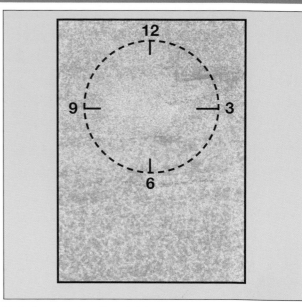

Think of a circle as being like a clock face

Emma finds she can ride Immi in canter with one hand, as long as she keeps her inside rein short enough

LIGHTENING THE FOREHAND – FLISS GILLOTT

With a horse that is heavy on the forehand, it can take several months of careful work to improve self-carriage. However, if a horse is heavy in your hand, it usually means that you are allowing him to be heavy. He cannot lean on something that is not there. Remember, when you ask with the hand, he should respond. Equally, when you ask with the leg, he should go forwards. The key words are 'forwards' and 'straight', meaning straight within himself, with the quarters following the shoulders.

You cannot hurry the process of lightening the forehand without risk of injury or putting a horse right off his work. The important thing is to be content with a steady improvement in your horse's way of going. It is vital that you don't allow him to go badly just so that he can keep going for longer. For example, if your horse is happy going along on his forehand for 45 minutes but is only able to work in proper balance for 10 minutes, then do 10 minutes in proper balance and give him a break. Quality is far more important than quantity.

Specific exercises for engaging the hocks focus around transitions and circle work. Transitions can be performed within the gaits as well as between gaits. Slow the trot for a few strides until he becomes soft in your hand, for example, before sending him forwards again from your leg. Take him on to the occasional small circle, keeping him upright on his legs (not motor-biking), maintaining a steady rhythm, looking for that softness in the hand again.

Rhythm is all-important. If he is heavy on his shoulders, he will almost certainly benefit from slowing the rhythm in both trot and canter, so that when you ride him forwards, he steps under with more impulsion rather than simply quickening his steps.

Always bear in mind that if your schooling is producing a negative result, then quite simply, your input is at fault. Be prepared to respond to your horse just as you expect him to respond to you.

Careful, consistent schooling is required to help a horse achieve self-carriage

Emma found it quite difficult to turn Immi with one hand to start with – the mare drifted to the outside. But once she slowed a little and became more attentive, things got better and Emma was able to keep a circle.

You have to be really patient with a horse that wants to bowl on all the time. The worst thing you can do is get stronger in the hand, because the one thing that causes a horse to run on is a rider pulling against it.

I asked Emma to decrease the size of her circles, still with both reins held in the outside hand, and advised her that on a smaller circle you need to half-halt and turn more often. You must also be sure that your inside rein is short enough to make the turn.

I suggested Emma drop her inside arm down by her side, so there was no temptation to take hold of the inside rein. I told her this would help her posture, too. Emma had to turn her hips, keep her weight into her inside stirrup, and use her outside leg to help the horse turn.

Canter control

I asked Emma to ride similar exercises in canter, progressing from riding around the outside of the arena with her reins in a single bridge, to a circle with a single bridge, and finally, one-handed around the circle.

I finished the lesson with another good balancing exercise for the horse: to canter across the diagonal and trot as you reach the opposite side of the school. When you first teach a horse to do this, you'll find they run on to the forehand, but with time their balance will improve.

Long and low

All this was quite hard work, and Immi was starting to get tired and wanted to stretch her neck. As it was the end of the session I was keen that she cooled off slowly, so I told Emma that it was quite OK to let her work low. When the horse gets tired, allow him to take a longer contact – but never before, otherwise you'll be carrying the horse.

The pair finish off by working long and low

CHRIS'S BALANCING DOS AND DON'TS

DO
- Practise riding around the outside of the school, staying in the same rhythm.
- Make transitions at specific markers and see how light on the contact you can keep your horse.
- Have your reins in a single bridge, with the reins in the outside hand.
- Give your horse a pat on the neck with the inside hand to help him relax.

DON'T
- Hold on to a horse that is running off with you. Instead, make half-halts, or ride him on a small circle, or make a downward transition.
- Lose your patience. If you do, you will take a big step backwards with your horse's training.
- Trawl endlessly round and round the school with a horse that's on the forehand. Correct it and start again.

Don't hold on to a horse that is running on to the forehand. Instead, do plenty of half-halts to stop this happening

Softly does it – Lee Pearson

Aim To teach a horse to soften and work forwards

I started Rachel and Charlie in walk to settle and relax Charlie, who was a little excited to be in a new place. I told Rachel to make lots of small circles using inside flexion to get him to listen. She made a few small circles, and Charlie began to soften and drop his nose, which was good. I told her to be sure she patted him as soon as he softened and dropped. Rachel continued to make small circles, and Charlie began to relax and listen more. I told Rachel to keep her body upright, and not to lean in! Also to establish the outline on one rein first, and to pat him the moment he 'gave'.

I stressed the importance of rewarding Charlie when he responded and softened through his neck and mouth. The moment the horse gives, you should reward him with a pat, use your voice, or straighten him out and go large. But the moment he fights and stiffens, go back to those circles and re-establish the soft, relaxed outline. I had plenty of praise for Charlie, who was really willing for such a big horse.

Rachel took my advice on board, and as Charlie softened, she rode him large around the arena. I advised her to ride him forwards in a marching walk: you should always ride forwards, be positive with your commands, and let the horse know when he's done well.

> **AT THIS MASTERCLASS**
>
> *Rachel Massie* started riding two years ago when she bought *Charlie*, who is her first horse. She enjoys dressage, hacking, cross-country and jumping. 'I like doing a bit of everything, really!' she told me. Charlie is a whopping 18hh! He is six years old, and ¾ Thoroughbred, ¼ Irish Draught. 'He's like a giant gymkhana pony,' Rachel said. 'He can be very argumentative when he wants to be!'

Charlie begins to relax and soften, bringing his head down

Transition, transition, transition!

When Rachel had established a forward-going walk and Charlie had relaxed through his neck and mouth, I moved the lesson on to the next stage – introducing transitions. Charlie was sufficiently warmed up, so the next task was to see how round Rachel could get him by working him down and forwards into the hand and by carrying out plenty of transitions from walk into trot.

I pointed out that when making transitions, Rachel needed to keep Charlie working around her inside leg to maintain the softness. And I told her not to be afraid to wake him up with a kick if he was being lazy and sluggish. I also advised her that if Charlie stiffened and came above the bit when moving into trot, she should try the following exercise:

- After a few strides in trot, walk again and regain the softness and acceptance of the bit.
- Walk a few strides, maintaining the softness, then ask for trot again.
- Repeat if the horse stiffens again in trot, until softness through the transition, as well as in the trot, is achieved and maintained.

After Rachel had done this exercise several times, Charlie began to soften in trot as well as in walk, and I encouraged Rachel to reward him with a longer rein. He had a good stretch

> ### USE YOUR VOICE
>
> Lee had this good advice: 'Keep using your voice to relax and unblock the horse, and don't let him evade your aids by going sideways. A horse is much more pleasurable to ride if he's soft, round and working actively forwards.'

while I chatted with Rachel; I advised her to put her leg on more when asking for forward movement, and to really think of pushing his bum up into her hands.

I also suggested that Rachel should think of a bigger, more forward trot when making transitions. Charlie sometimes became a bit sluggish in the walk-to-trot transitions, and I reminded Rachel that the more you lose the energy, the more you will lose the battle.

Charlie started protesting at these stronger aids in the transitions, and put in small bucks as Rachel squeezed her legs around him; so I recommended she slowed down to walk and made him soften again: if the horse bucks, you should make him soften, because he won't find it so easy to buck while he's being bent to the inside!

After a few strides in trot, Rachel makes a transition to walk to keep Charlie listening to her

Charlie protests about Rachel's firmer leg aids

When Charlie had settled again, he really began to use his hindquarters. I noticed that his overtrack (when the horse's hind hoofprints land in front of the hoofprints left by the forelegs) was a good 30cm (12in) when he was going forwards, showing that he was engaged through his back end. I also pointed out to Rachel that he had stopped poking his tongue out, and that he had a nice froth building up, which is a good indication of a horse's acceptance of the contact. I suggested Rachel reward him with a long, low stretch, while working smaller circles into her larger ones.

Working on canter

After his stretch, Rachel picked Charlie up into a higher outline and worked him large around the arena. He was stiffer on the right rein and still a little spooky. To help this, I told her to bend him using the inside rein, but without snatching at the rein or he'd go dead to her aids. Rachel asked quietly, and sure enough, Charlie started to soften around the next corner.

To do this you should gently play with the horse's mouth with your fingers while applying the inside leg, then apply both legs and keep his neck straight. In Charlie's case, this should keep him soft down the long sides, too. In fact he was still quite unsettled on the long side and spooked again.

I instructed Rachel to really ride him forwards into the bridle! As she did so, he began to take up a more relaxed, rhythmic and settled trot, at which point I suggested she make an upward transition to canter. As she asked Charlie forwards into canter, he responded to her legs by softening and bending. I was pleased, and told her to pat him! Then to bring him forwards to trot as a reward, keep him forwards, then canter again.

Charlie came slightly above the bit, so Rachel softened her inside rein as she brought him forwards to trot. I encouraged her to keep the trot active so she could canter again, and warned her not to let him get behind the leg.

Rachel made several transitions from trot to canter, while I reminded her to talk to him and to keep the canter forwards. Charlie began cantering on the wrong leg, but I pushed them on, making them stay on a smaller circle and telling her not to worry about the wrong leg, he'd correct it if he wanted to and he'd learn in future to use the correct leg – don't let him have a break just because he's not on the correct leg, but keep going forwards. He was still a little strong, but I advised Rachel to use the energy to her advantage and to keep riding him forwards.

I continued to ask Rachel to make plenty of transitions from trot to canter, and back again, and reminded her to keep herself, as well as Charlie, active in both trot and canter. I also advised her to ride more on the inside rein when carrying out smaller circles. It's better to let the horse find his own balance in the transitions – don't block his front end.

Charlie still occasionally took off on the wrong leg in canter, but this was his mistake, and I told Rachel to keep him cantering. After several transitions, Charlie found his balance and began to strike off on the correct leading leg every time.

To re-establish a soft outline, Rachel works smaller circles into larger ones

Cooling off

To finish, Rachel walked, trotted and cantered on a long, loose rein to allow Charlie to stretch through his back and neck. I reminded her that even though she was cooling him down, she should keep his flexion to the inside, and make sure he stretched properly on both reins.

This was Rachel's second lesson with me, and I thought Charlie had improved since last time – he was much fitter, and we did a lot more with him. He needs to think forwards all the time, and that way he won't retaliate so much!

RACHEL'S VERDICT

'By the end of the lesson, I felt elated, as Charlie was working in a lovely outline and was really listening to my aids. Lee has taught me several different methods of achieving an outline, including transitions and riding circles, and I can use them in future schooling sessions to continue to improve. I feel the lessons with Lee have really brought Charlie and me together.'

Charlie discovers it is easier to canter on the correct lead

Hot stuff – Emile Faurie

Aim To help a stressed horse to relax and be able to work well

I asked Jan to show me a few circles in trot and canter so I could assess their strengths and weaknesses.

After watching Cecil bowling on around the arena with his ground-eating stride, I commented to Jan that he really *was* a hot potato – he'd got fabulous paces, but he needed to chill out a bit and learn to work in a more consistent rhythm: at the moment he wants to go as fast as he can, with his legs up round his ears and his head tucked between his front legs. The trouble is, when a horse like this charges off, you feel you need to take more of a hold and then he becomes even more overbent. I told Jan to let him trot a little longer on a circle to give him time to get used to the unfamiliar surroundings, then hopefully he'd start to relax.

After a few minutes Cecil did start to relax more, and as a result he began to work with a more even stride and in a more consistent rhythm. I asked Jan to bring him forwards to walk so I could talk her through some useful relaxation exercises.

AT THIS MASTERCLASS

Jan Chopping has had *Cecil* for almost two years, and told us it was love at first sight. Cecil is a seven-year-old Oldenburg gelding. Jan says that when she first got him he was wild. 'He could buck more than any horse has bucked before,' she says.

Cecil alternates between staying calm and relaxed and becoming tense and overbent

Cecil has lots of muscle at the top of his neck, and not so much in front of the wither; this is because of his habitual way of going

In canter Cecil is pulling himself forwards with his front legs and Jan's riding becomes defensive

What a difference when Jan uses more leg and less hand in canter

Trot, trust and praise

I asked Jan to come forwards to trot again, explaining the importance of rewarding your horse as soon as he does as you ask him to. If you are really consistent with your praise, then your training will improve much quicker because your horse is clearer about what you do and what you don't want him to do. And it doesn't have to be a huge pat on the neck – even

saying 'good boy' in a calm tone is enough for the horse to understand he's done the right thing.

But when they went back to work in trot, Cecil reverted to charging, with his front legs up by his ears and his head coming further and further behind the vertical, which made Jan take more of a hold of him. I reminded her not to grab hold of the

As the pair begin to work in trot, Cecil can't resist the temptation to charge off

front end, but to ride him just like she did in canter, lifting the hands to lift the poll and using the leg to activate the hindlegs.

I told Jan she would have to learn to trust Cecil a bit more – and then he'd trust her more, too. I know she feels a bit out of control, but if every time he rushes off she pulls on the reins, things will never improve. I advised that if he went too fast, to use a smaller circle to slow him down. And if he still felt too fast, to ride a transition to walk, re-balance and then trot again.

I suggested that she could also try using a voice command when she asks for a downward transition; that way the horse learns to associate a *word* with what you want him to do, and you won't have to use as much rein contact. I teach all my horses to do transitions from the voice at a very early age because if you're subtle enough, you can use this command very quietly in your test, too, which acts as a 'security blanket'.

At first things didn't go very smoothly, and whenever Jan lifted her hands slightly in the trot to encourage Cecil not to tuck his head behind the vertical, he cantered. I advised her that I'd be inclined to let him canter if he wanted to, and then ride him in the same way in canter. That way he'd learn that he can't use cantering as an evasion.

Again I stressed the importance of being quick to praise, and pointed out that you can reward a horse by backing off when he does what you want. So you ask by sitting deep, using your legs and lifting the hands, and when the horse lifts his poll, sits behind more and becomes light, you reward by doing nothing.

TURNING POINT

Jan and Cecil have problems riding accurate circles. 'He's got such a long stride that to ride an accurate 20m circle, I feel as if I have to keep my turning aids in gear all the time, otherwise we go straight for too long,' Jan explained to me.

'Then that's exactly what you need to do!' I replied. 'Every stride, think turn. If you feel that you've asked him to turn and he isn't responding, turn the upper half of your body and bring both hands slightly to the inside. Remember to use your outside aids to turn as well as your inside ones.'

Confidence building

There was a moment where Cecil shifted his balance and brought his head out from his chest, but panicked when he did so and shot forwards. I reassured Jan that a lot of her work would be in building confidence with this horse, because he gets in a panic and then everything blows his brain. You almost want him to come into the school sighing a bit, rather than how he is at the moment, which is stressed most of the time.

I pointed out that Cecil has quite an 'uphill' build and therefore shouldn't find it particularly difficult to take his weight back. At the moment he is choosing to work on the forehand, so he needs to learn to carry himself a bit more, rather than relying on his rider to carry him.

After a while Cecil did relax more, and I was able to reassure Jan that it looked better, that he looked softer through his jaw, and not as if she was having a constant battle with him. And for the first time in this session he was swinging through his back!

Emile's advice

My advice was for Jan to ride lots of transitions every time she schooled Cecil, as this would help him to become more regular in his work. His movement is very impressive, but it isn't always correct – it's not 'real'. *Real* is when the horse relaxes and works in a consistent rhythm.

I advised keeping him out in the field 24/7 so he learns to switch off. I did that with one of my top horses, Livello, who had a tendency to be fizzy and stressy, and it really worked for him.

I told her to try to keep his mind occupied, and teach him to wait for his commands, rather than letting him take charge.

Calm, repetitive work has paid off and Cecil begins to respond well

HOW IT WAS FOR JAN

'A few weeks before my lesson with Emile I couldn't even ride a canter/trot transition with this horse. I was desperately in need of another stepping-stone, and Emile gave me that. He showed me how to encourage Cecil to raise his poll and work over his back and into a more secure contact.

'I have since learnt that Cecil gets even more stressed when competing. He will do many things without a second thought, but as soon as we turn down the centre line in a test he goes into overdrive, head down and legs everywhere! His marks are not important at this stage, but my ambition is to take him to Grand Prix, and I'm certain that if we take it slowly we will get there, and enjoy the journey as well.'

Showing submission – Emile Faurie

Aim To help a horse learn the right outline for dressage by activating the hindquarters

I asked Sally-Anne to show me a few minutes of trot and canter on both reins, so I could make an assessment. When she had done so I told her that according to the *Pony Club Manual*, her leathers were too long! This was making her feet slide too far into the stirrups, which was upsetting her balance and tipping her forwards at times.

I explained that there is this strong myth that dressage riders must ride with really long stirrups, but in actual fact you should ride with your stirrups at a length that allows you to stay central in the saddle and keep your balance.

While Sally-Anne put her stirrups up a hole, I told her what I felt about Squidge. I thought he was a smart-looking horse, but tended to lack suppleness through his poll, which was causing him to hollow a bit. Also, Sally-Anne tended to ride him with the leg on all the time to keep him thinking forwards.

I suggested that if I prodded her gently non-stop she wouldn't notice much, but if I gave her a harder prod every five minutes she'd notice much more, so told her to try to adopt that philosophy when she was riding. That way Squidge would learn to keep *himself* going forwards, rather than rely on her.

Sally-Anne's stirrup leathers are too long, which is putting her out of balance

Circle in canter

As canter was the pace that Sally-Anne was finding most difficult with Squidge, I asked her to ride a 20m circle in canter. I advised her to let her legs hang nice and relaxed, and when Squidge dropped behind the leg, to give him one big kick to send him on, then relax the leg again.

While Sally-Anne was practising this, I gave her something else to think about, too. I told her she needed to get Squidge more relaxed through his poll by flexing him a little to the outside and then to the inside again. To do this you use your wrists to flex him, not your arms, otherwise you'll pull on the bars of his mouth, which will draw his head down – and potentially hurt his mouth.

Sally-Anne had a lot to think about, so I reminded her to give him a kick if he dropped behind the leg, then to flex him to the outside a little, then to the inside to improve the submission. When you flex a horse like this, be sure he bends properly through his neck and doesn't tilt his head – and open the rein, don't pull back. Then half-halt to stop him dropping his head too low and going on to the forehand. Ride him forwards into the half-halt rather than pulling on the reins. You want to get the horse's hindquarters more underneath him, so he takes more weight behind and lightens his forehand.

The result was a more submissive and forward-thinking Squidge, and a rider who didn't need to use her legs every stride. I told Sally-Anne that they were looking good; as riders we should constantly be thinking about what we can do to improve how our horse is going. Ask yourself: 'Is he forwards enough? Is he round enough? Is his forehand light? Perhaps you need to half-halt or ride a circle to rebalance?' Never think, 'This will do', because it can always be better!

Squidge and Sally-Anne work on their canter

Bringing the energy from back to front

One thing I stressed to Sally-Anne was how important it is to think of riding the horse from the back to the front, particularly through downward transitions and half-halts. It's important to have the power coming from the hindquarters and to ride the horse forwards into a contact, because if you *pull* your horse into an outline with the reins, the hindlegs will go further out behind him.

After a quick breather, I asked Sally-Anne to pick up the reins and walk on – but then I called out to her to drop them again, and told her that when she took them up the next time, she should pick them up more gradually. On the first occasion she took up an immediate contact, really suddenly, which made the horse go behind the vertical and back off the leg.

I demonstrated the effect I wanted Sally-Anne to achieve, using a whip, which I bent upwards. I explained that if you think of pushing the back end underneath the horse like this, then you can see what happens: the horse's back comes up, and he rounds his outline.

Improving sitting trot

I wanted Sally-Anne to work on her sitting trot a little, to help her seat and improve her balance. To do this I told her to take a big, deep breath in as she sat, then to gradually let it out again, to help her relax. Then you allow your lower back to swing, let go with your seat, and don't tense your body – anywhere!

I then asked Sally-Anne to gradually increase the rhythm to get Squidge in front of the leg again. I explained to her that he had dropped behind the leg as soon as she went to sitting trot, so she needed to 'rev' him up again. Sally-Anne found it hard to keep Squidge going forwards, so I suggested she substitute her big kick for a tap with the whip. If you feel your horse drop behind the leg, tap him with the whip instead of kicking, then you'll be able to keep concentrating on your sitting trot.

From a more forward-going sitting trot, I asked Sally-Anne to ride a transition to canter, keeping the forward rhythm throughout the transition and into the canter. Now she had a much better rhythm.

Just to add to her list of things to think about, I added that at that moment in time her circles looked more like squares! Circles don't have any corners, so don't ride any part of the circle straight. In fact, think of angling your horse slightly to the inside of the circle all the time so you're constantly turning him.

Pushing the horse's back end underneath him rounds his back and therefore his whole outline – I demonstrate this with a whip

Squidge isn't working through from behind. He is a bit hollow in his outline, his hindquarters are trailing and he isn't in front of Sally Anne's leg aids – look at the area behind the saddle

Sally-Anne works harder on Squidge's way of going and he begins to track up (his hind footprints follow in the footprints of the fore feet), he's showing a rounder outline and taking bigger steps – again, look at the area behind the saddle, and at his feet

---

EMILE'S ADVICE

- Always think of riding the back end of the horse to the front end, not the other way round.
- Think about what you can do to improve your horse's way of going while you're riding.
- Use half-halts to re-balance, if necessary.

- Open the rein to flex the horse but never pull back on it.
- Use corners to help with engagement.
- You'll pick up extra marks in tests by riding accurate shapes and circles.

Forwards to canter and corners

I asked Sally-Anne to make a right lead canter transition from walk, telling her to sit up, look up, keep her hands low, to flex Squidge slightly to the inside to help with roundness, and then canter! She did this well, so I instructed her to canter across the short diagonal and then to keep him in counter canter around the short side of the arena.

I wanted Sally-Anne to keep Squidge flexed right in the counter canter. In a test situation he'd need to be straighter in the counter canter, but you need to flex the horse more when you're schooling as it will help to keep him rounder.

Another schooling exercise I showed Sally-Anne was using corners to improve the canter. It's really simple, but you'll be amazed how many riders don't ride into their corners. For this exercise you need to shorten your reins, sit on your seat,

and keep the horse's hindlegs active by using your legs. As you approach the corner, step into your inside leg and use it to push him into the corner more. The corner helps to get the hindlegs stepping under more, so the horse takes more weight on to his hindlegs and lightens his forehand. Use every corner to your benefit – they are really useful!

As a test of good submission, I wanted to see that Sally-Anne could give both reins away in canter and that Squidge would to stay soft. I asked her to flex Squidge to the inside before giving away the reins. If you give the rein and your horse stays round and in the same rhythm, rather than breaking into trot or charging off with his head in the air, then the chances are you have him in good submission, so you can try this as a test from time to time.

Flex and stretch

I wanted Sally-Anne and Squidge to finish the session with some stretching. I always work my horses on a longer contact at the end of their schooling sessions, as it helps them to unwind and cools down the muscles gently. I also asked Sally-Anne to come forwards to rising trot, to ride forwards and to keep flexing Squidge a little to the inside.

However, I advised her not to overdo the flexing, otherwise you put the horse off balance, then he'll fall on his shoulder to try and secure his hindleg. Instead, just keep opening the inside hand towards the centre of the school slightly by using a subtle wrist action. Sally-Anne did this well, and I congratulated her because Squidge was really starting to 'give' to her.

Squidge has a tendency to hollow his outline in counter canter, so I asked Sally-Anne to keep him flexed

Giving the reins away makes Squidge hollow a little but he stays in the same rhythm, showing good submission

Squidge enjoys a stretch at the end of the lesson

SALLY-ANNE'S VERDICT

'I really liked the fact that Emile worked on the basics. He actually apologized at the end of the lesson for keeping it basic, but I was pleased about that. After all, you can't ride all the tricks if the basics aren't there! I realize how important the basics are, and how much time even the top riders have to spend perfecting them.

'I really enjoyed my lesson with Emile and he gave me a lot of very useful tips. He showed me that to achieve good results you have to really ride your horse. Dressage isn't all about sitting pretty. You have to work at it!'

Bend and flex – Christopher Bartle

Aim To teach a horse to be supple and relaxed using half-pass to leg yield

A horse like Kaboom needs lots of reassurance from his rider – and from his trainer – during schooling sessions. I explained to Richard that it is important to keep a horse like this on our side, because as soon as he works against us, we are fighting a losing battle. The only way a horse can be physically relaxed is to be mentally relaxed first, so that's what we aim for with any horse we are training.

I have a sand track around the outside of my cross-country course and outdoor school, and use it regularly for schooling my horses. I find it is a less intense environment to work them out on the track. As soon as you bring a horse into the school, it is a bit like putting them in an exam situation, and the more chilled we can keep the work, the better it is for the horse.

Many riders find it hard to keep their horse straight, particularly when they are doing lateral work – the horse tries to fall out through a shoulder or swing the hindquarters. To help with this, think of riding your horse along a corridor. Your reins and legs are the sides of the corridor and your horse must travel in the middle, whether he is going in a straight line or moving sideways.

Richard and Kaboom work on the corridor exercise

Learning the exercise

I asked Richard to start on a small left circle in trot and to practise getting more inside flexion from Kaboom. I explained that in order to get more inside bend, you need to release the outside rein more, otherwise you're blocking the inside bend. From this exaggerated inside bend, I asked Richard to ride half-pass across the diagonal, initially keeping inside bend, but gradually changing the bend so eventually the horse was in outside bend, making the half-pass become a leg yield. The exercise finished with a 10m circle right and was repeated with half-pass and leg yield back the other way.

This exercise is helpful because even if your horse isn't fully established in half-pass and leg yield, you can start by simply changing his direction of bend, and then progress to the full exercise when he is ready.

Whenever Richard took sitting trot during this exercise, Kaboom tried to canter, so I suggested that Richard ride the whole exercise in sitting trot. I pointed out that at the higher levels of dressage, you have to sit to the trot, so the horse has to get used to it. I asked Richard to ride Kaboom with a longer neck, in a slightly more stretched outline. I wanted the horse to balance himself, rather than him leaning on the contact and being held up by Richard; with a longer neck he will learn to find his own balance. Kaboom was a bit tense at first, but started to relax once he understood what Richard wanted.

Richard also found that Kaboom was leaning on his right rein, so to prevent this I told him to stop and ride a turn on the forehand to the right until the horse was light, then go again.

Starting the exercise in half-pass

Changing the bend has made Kaboom a bit tense

Kaboom settles into doing a good leg yield

Working in canter

I then asked for the half-pass to leg-yield exercise in canter. I wanted Richard to start by riding a 10m circle in canter (you can make the circle larger if your horse isn't balanced enough), then go into half-pass right, slowly changing the bend into leg yield. On reaching the opposite side of the arena, I told Richard to stay in counter canter but keep inside bend, as if he were still in the leg-yield position. I explained that this was a good exercise for setting the horse up for a flying change before actually asking for it, because when you ride a flying change, you alter the bend before asking for the change. This exercise is good for this horse because as soon as you alter the bend with Kaboom, he thinks that you are going to ask him for a flying change and often does one anyway. Hopefully this exercise will teach him that we don't always want him to change.

I reminded Richard that the exercise is also more about giving with the outside rein when you change to the leg yield, rather than taking with the inside rein. The rider has to be brave and allow the outside rein forwards, and use the outside leg, not the outside rein, to support the horse's outside shoulder. The inside leg is the dominant leg in leg yield and half-pass, and the outside leg is the supporting leg.

Kaboom starts off well in the canter half-pass, but does a flying change instead of simply changing the direction of bend

Long and low

I am a great believer in stretching work to relax the horse both physically and mentally. When I work my own horses, I vary between riding them in what I call a 'test outline' and doing stretching work. But whichever outline the horse is in, he must keep the same rhythm and balance.

Throughout the session I gave Richard and Kaboom regular stretching breaks, and to encourage Kaboom to stretch more,

I asked Richard to imagine he was allowing the horse to drink from a bucket on the floor. And if the horse doesn't want to stretch more, try sitting further back in the saddle. When the rider's weight is further back, the horse has to stretch his neck to balance himself. It's a really useful exercise for horses that have short necks and try to curl up on the rider all the time.

Allow the horse plenty of opportunities to stretch and relax

AIDS FOR A FLYING CHANGE

I advise teaching your horse to do a flying change under the guidance of an instructor that you trust, but here's an idea of how to ask for one.

- First of all, you need to know that your horse is ready, and a good indication of this is that he is balanced in counter canter on both reins (that is, his rhythm doesn't change and he doesn't plough on to the forehand), and that you can ask for each canter lead in a straight line.
- Many trainers teach flying change by cantering across the diagonal, slowly changing the flexion at the poll but keeping the horse in the corridor feeling – between hand and leg.
- Before you ask for the change, ask the horse to come into the new inside bend, then take your new outside leg back and new inside leg slightly forwards – make sure you maintain the pressure with it. Don't lean into the change, as this encourages the horse to change his front legs first.

Move your new outside leg (here the left one) back to ask for the change

The finishing touches

Kaboom still felt strong in Richard's right hand, so I had a sit on him to work out what was happening. I could feel the problem straightaway: Kaboom was locking on to the right rein, and when you tried to give it away, he was falling out to the right. He was totally ignoring my right leg.

To rectify this I rode a turn on the forehand to the right, and then once the horse was light again, repeated the half-pass to leg-yield exercise to the right. Kaboom resisted, so I walked him and repeated the turn-on-the-forehand exercise. Kaboom soon started to feel lighter in the right rein, and I was able to half-pass and leg yield him all the way across the diagonal. However, when he got to the opposite side of the arena, Kaboom still wouldn't allow me to keep him in counter canter with inside bend, and kept doing a flying change instead.

When the horse does a change that I don't want, I will pretend I wanted it, so it doesn't turn into a big deal. Then I ask myself what I did wrong and have another go. It's always better to look for the positive, and the positive thing here is that this horse gave me a lovely, clean change.

When I tried the exercise again with Kaboom, we got better results, and so I repeated it a few times, to get the idea clear in the horse's mind. If it felt as though Kaboom was going to make a change, I made a walk transition before it happened, then quickly released the right rein and gave him a pat down the right side of his neck. The pat is for two reasons: first, to help the horse relax; and second, to force me to let go of the right rein, because the tendency for me is to want to hold on to it.

On our final attempt at this exercise, I rewarded Kaboom by allowing him to do what he wanted to do – a flying change – and the result was a good one. I explained to Richard that he'd been dying to do it, so it would have been mean not to have let him. Even so, the horse has to learn that he changes when you ask him to, but not otherwise. He should let you set him up as though you were asking for a change, but not change until you actually give the command.

After a turn on the forehand, I use half pass to leg yield to lighten Kaboom on the right rein

TIPS FOR SUCCESS

Remember you are training your horse both physically and mentally, so you should try to keep everything as relaxed as possible.

- When you take with one rein, you have to give with the other (photo below) otherwise you are blocking the amount of bend the horse can give. And a pat with the giving hand is a good idea, too.

- If you are preparing your horse for learning flying changes, ride the half-pass to leg-yield exercise, first in trot – or even walk – and progress to canter, once the horse is ready. You should find that once he can do this exercise calmly in canter, and stay in balance, he will be ready to try a change.

- Vary your 'test outline' work with stretching work and encourage the horse to stretch by taking your bodyweight further back in the saddle.

- Alternate riding both rising and sitting trot. From Elementary level onwards in dressage you have to sit to the trot throughout a test, so both horse and rider need to get used to it.

- Don't make a big deal out of mistakes or you will simply cause your horse stress. Come forwards to walk, think about it and how you can correct it, and then do it again.

As a reward I finally ask Kaboom for a flying change, which he performs quite beautifully

On a bend, always give with the outside rein to allow your horse to do what you are asking

Create a great topline – Christopher Bartle

Aim To use stretching work to increase a horse's suppleness and agility and improve self-carriage

AT THIS MASTERCLASS

Magnus Gallerdal is a Swedish event rider who is based at the Yorkshire Riding Centre. He has ridden at major events, including Badminton, and he was 17th at the Athens Olympics with *Keymaster*, a stunning 13-year-old Thoroughbred gelding who was originally bred for the racecourse. Keymaster's other successes include finishing 7th at Luhmuhlen and 9th at Pau.

I do strongly believe that creating a supple, agile horse that carries himself, rather than relying on his rider to carry him, is achieved only through good schooling. To achieve this aim it is important to be consistent – for example, you must make all your aids the same. Aim to have your horse sharp to your aids, by using firmer aids when he doesn't listen to subtle ones. Be consistent with your expectations – don't allow your horse to give you sloppy upward transitions some of the time, then tell him off for them another time.

Keymaster has a good, consistent outline in all his paces and is trained to Advanced level in dressage. However, as I watched the pair warm up, I felt that the horse was a little tight in his neck. He sets his neck in a good position for dressage, but then if you want him to move it somewhere else – that is, if you ask him to stretch a little – he doesn't want to. For some riders, getting their horse to stretch is easier said than done, and Magnus was struggling to get good stretching from Keymaster.

Teaching a horse to stretch

However, I had some tips that I thought would help, and told Magnus to start with a short rein and work the horse a little 'up'. In this situation you should try to keep the horse active (but not rushing), and in a good rhythm and balance, gradually allowing him a little more rein. The key is only to give him as much rein as he will take, which may be as little as an inch at a time. And if he doesn't take the rein forwards, then take that little amount back again.

You must be careful not to pull back on the reins, and don't try to bring his head down with your hands, either. Stretching must be the horse's idea. I also advised riding this exercise on a circle, as circling helps with balance, and encourages better stretching than riding in a straight line.

Counter balance

I had a sit on Keymaster to play a little with the stretching, and when I had him in a longer frame, I varied his exercises to include some counter canter. Keymaster was a bit stilted in this pace, and I considered it was because he loses balance a little in the counter canter, as he's waiting for his rider to help him. But

Keymaster begins work a little tight in the neck and reluctant to stretch

I wasn't going to support him – he has to find his own balance. I suggested to Magnus that he should do lots of counter canter in a stretched outline with Keymaster – he would really benefit from it.

Lowering the neck

Keymaster was still showing reluctance to lengthen his whole frame and stretch out, so I described another exercise, which I find often works well for horses like Keymaster. This exercise comes from a French expression *descente d'encolure,* which translated literally means 'lowering of the neck'. And you train the horse to do it by lifting your reins a bit higher, as this helps to create more submission. Anyone who sees me schooling youngsters will notice that I sometimes put my index finger underneath the rein and lift it up for a moment, then once the horse gives to me, I remove my finger.

Magnus got some good results from this exercise and Keymaster started to show some proper stretching. I advised Magnus that Keymaster needed to do lots of this sort of work to free him up. Although he works well, he is tight through his back and neck, and he relies on his rider to hold him up a bit too much. Lots of stretching work will not only give you a more supple horse, but also one that can carry himself – in other words, one with established good self-carriage.

GET IN POSITION

Magnus told me that sometimes he feels as though he is stuck against the saddle. I advised him it was important to ride with a loose thigh, so every time he felt clamped, to come forwards to walk, take his lower leg away from the horse for a few seconds to open the hip and relax the thigh, then carry on again. If the rider is not nice and loose on the horse's back, then you can't expect the horse to be loose and free in his way of going.

I added that having ridden in Magnus' saddle, I found there wasn't much room for my seat, so suggested that a saddle with more room for his seat would allow him to be looser.

Magnus loosens up his thighs and hips by taking his lower leg away

Counter canter in a stretched outline encourages Keymaster to find his own balance

Lifting the reins to ask Keymaster to lower his head

Making circles

To further improve Keymaster's self-carriage and to encourage him to stretch, I asked Magnus to come on to a 10m circle in canter. Once a horse is comfortable with 10m circles, this is a very good exercise to try. Keymaster was established enough to do this exercise in canter; however, with a horse that isn't, you should stick to trot.

When you work a horse in a small, confined area, you are constantly turning him and asking for his hindleg to step more under his body. This encourages the horse to take more weight behind, which puts him into better self-carriage – and this, in itself, often leads to better stretching. And if you find it hard to stay on a 10m circle, then mark out a square using four poles.

One thing I must say is that it is really important never to overdo the small circle work. It is hard for the horse to work on a small circle, so ride a few small circles, then at a good moment ride a few bigger ones, then come back to the small one again.

I had one last – but very important – tip for Magnus for riding good, accurate 10m circles: always try to avoid pulling the horse around with the inside rein. Instead, concentrate more on the outside of the horse, so you are encouraged to use your outside aids more to turn him. This means that you avoid having too much inside bend, and a horse that falls out through the outside shoulder.

Self-carriage trick

I finished the lesson by showing Magnus a very simple exercise that I find can help with anything new you try. By positioning your horse in shoulder-fore before you do something new, you set him up for the next movement, as it brings his inside hindleg underneath him more and puts him into better self-carriage. So even before you make an upward or a downward transition with your horse, ask him for a little shoulder-fore position. You'll really feel him step through more from behind! I demonstrated this theory on Keymaster by riding shoulder-fore before starting some half pirouettes in walk, and it really helped. I explained that shoulder-fore is a great preparation exercise for a pirouette because it puts the horse in the correct position before you start! (For more information on shoulder-fore, see pp.22–23.)

Keymaster responds well to the canter exercise and starts to work in good self-carriage

GOOD SCHOOLING

- Try to vary your schooling sessions. I like to loosen up the horse on a long rein for around 15 minutes, then I alternate between working him up together in a suitable outline for dressage and working him in a longer frame, to allow his muscles to stretch.
- Keep the horse in front of the leg at all times. Event horses, especially, can find dressage training a bit boring, and then they get lazy and the rider ends up doing most of the work. Try not to let this happen. Ask the horse to go forwards, then back off him when he does as you ask, but be quick to remind him to go again when you need to.
- Always think about your riding and position. Make things as easy as you can for your horse by staying light in the saddle, and by making sure you're not tightening his back by clamping your legs too tightly against his sides.
- Be consistent with your training.
- Never lose your temper with your horse, or blame him for something that might have been your fault. Remember to work with him and keep him on your side. Reward him when he does as you ask (this helps him to learn quicker), but when he doesn't do as you ask, check you are asking clearly, then ask again more positively.

The hard work pays off and Keymaster is much more relaxed in his neck

Fine tuning – Carl Hester

Aim To increase activity in the hindquarters and work on canter pirouettes

If you've taken a horse up through the levels of a discipline, as Judi has with Arnie, you're likely to have formed a strong relationship with him. 'I love him to bits and know him inside out,' says Judi. 'I enjoy riding him, but feel I need to start asking more from him in order to improve my marks. But I need to know how!' Judi says of Arnie, 'He's always been a bit lazy with his hindlegs, and I think this is what is letting us down in some movements in the tests we do, particularly the pirouettes.'

AT THIS MASTERCLASS

Judi Foster resumed her riding career at 37 after giving up in her teens. At 41, she took her BHSAI and she is now a keen dressage rider. She has regular lessons with dressage trainer Helen Sissons, whom she says has helped her enormously.

Antonio (Arnie) is a 16.2hh 15-year-old Hanoverian gelding by Akzent II. He is working at Prix St Georges level – Judi took him up through the levels herself, so it's quite an achievement. Every year the combination has qualified for the regional dressage championships, and at Novice level they qualified for the national championships. Judi says: 'Arnie's biggest problems are that he is a worrier, and as a result can be tight through his back. Also, he can be lazy – he lacks impulsion in some movements.'

By sitting the canter back on Arnie's hindlegs, Judi is able to ask for a good halt transition

Starting with transitions

After they'd warmed up, I suggested Judi try an exercise that would help to shift the weight more on to the horse's hindlegs and off the forehand. We can only start to improve the pirouettes if the horse is carrying enough weight behind, so I told her to ride some canter-halt-canter transitions to help with this. When the horse is in halt, ask him to be softer through the neck by squeezing the reins gently with your fingers. Then, when he's 'let go', canter again.

As a general rule, if a horse can do good canter-halt-canter transitions – and by 'good' I mean that he shows no resistance through the reins, and that the transition is directly from canter to halt without any walk or trot in between – then he is carrying enough weight behind to start work on pirouettes.

I also instructed Judi that she needed to shorten the canter before she asked for the halt, as Arnie was inclined to fall on the forehand through the transition. You won't ever get a good halt transition from a canter which is even slightly on the forehand. Use half-halts (when you say walk with the reins, and with the legs say canter) to transfer the weight back. These subtle weight transfers should make your horse softer and lighter in your hand, and then you can make your transition to halt.

Judi tried what I suggested and got a good response from Arnie, which was really encouraging. I also reminded her that if he tried to break from canter, to touch him with her leg to send him on again.

One final point I wanted to make was that with a horse that is inclined to be a bit lazy, like Judi's, it was important not to start riding him 'hard'. You see it so often. The horse gets lazy, the rider works harder, the horse becomes more dead to the rider's leg and before you know it, you have a rider who's banging away with the legs and a horse that still isn't going forwards. So ask him forwards with the leg, say, every five strides, then sit quietly again. Only use the leg if you need it, and when he's going forwards, leave him alone. With lazy horses, less is always more.

Quarters-in

Next, I asked Judi to bring Arnie on to a 10m circle and ride him in travers (quarters-in – see pp.26–27). Again, this is a good way to lighten the forehand and get more engagement. I wanted Arnie's hindlegs to stay on about an 8m circle, and the front legs to stay on the 10m one.

I told Judi to ride a few circles in travers, and then to freshen him up by going large in a bigger canter, otherwise he might have started to clam up. I wanted him to stay forward-thinking at all times.

After riding this exercise on both reins, Judi gave Arnie a quick break, and then practised riding some transitions from collected to medium canter on a large circle. When you ask a horse to collect, gently tap him with your whip on the top of his hindquarters near the top of his tail, to encourage his hindquarters to lower. Make sure you sit on your outside seatbone and lighten your inside one, so that he can really step through with his inside hindleg.

I encouraged Judi to make Arnie bounce in the canter – I wanted him so collected I could walk beside him, but without losing the energy.

Judi and Arnie demonstrate an obedient travers

Perfect pirouettes

Now that Arnie was taking more weight behind in canter, I suggested they start working on pirouettes. I told Judi to ride a pirouette around me, to keep turning, to ride every stride and look towards me to help her turn. At home you can get someone to stand in the middle so you know how big or small you're riding pirouettes. And if you can't get a person, ride them around a cone or a jump wing.

As the pair started the movements, Arnie went flat again so I called out to Judi to go large for a moment and make adjustments to the canter tempo, to go medium, then collected. When they came back to the pirouettes, these were much better, so I suggested that she let Arnie walk and pat him as a reward.

I observed that as soon as Judi was 'off' Arnie's case he started to 'chill' again, so she had to be quick to recognize when he was being lazy and do something to get the energy back.

I use half-piaffe steps with my horses to create energy because it gets the hindlegs to work quicker. I told Judi to collect Arnie up in walk and take a feel on the reins to prevent his energy going out the front. You need to use your legs to gain more energy from the hindlegs, and if the horse doesn't listen, tap him with your whip on top of his hindquarters. Judi did as I suggested and Arnie performed some nice steps. When the horse does a few decent steps, walk and pat him. For a character like Arnie, if you can keep him a bit 'hot', like Judi had him in the half-piaffe, then you can make more expression in the other work.

Judi uses half-piaffe steps to get some energy and activity into Arnie's hindquarters

BANISHING TENSION

I noticed that Judi held on to the inside rein too much, and advised her that Arnie needed to be a lot lighter in her inside hand. A good way to stop a horse 'hanging' on the inside rein is to lift it and press it slightly against the neck. I suggested she try this and see what happened.

It worked really well for Judi. By lifting the rein against the neck, Arnie immediately softened more through his head and neck. I reminded her that as soon as he did so, she should return her hand to its normal position.

As well as being softer in Judi's inside hand, I wanted to see this horse relaxing his neck more just in front of the saddle. If you look at the pictures below, you can see that Arnie has lots of wrinkles there, which is a sign that he's not truly round through his topline. When you want to achieve a better outline, think of the horse rounding his back up into the saddle and stretching forwards into the rein contact. Never pull the horse's head and neck in with the reins.

Lift your inside rein up and against the neck slightly to achieve a lighter feel

Wrinkles in front of the saddle are a sign that Arnie could relax his neck more

When he's persuaded to stretch into the contact more the creases disappear

Concentrated corners

A dressage judge will always be much more impressed by a competitor who rides an accurate test. Riding to the markers and making good use of the corners looks so much more professional, and I noted that Judi could make better use of her corners, which would boost her test marks.

Riding good corners will not only get you better marks in a test, it will also help to engage the horse's inside hindleg. So, if you were coming around the corner and going straight into a medium or extended trot, for example, riding a good corner will set the horse up on the hindleg more, so that he pushes off his hindlegs into the bigger trot, rather than charging on to the forehand. I gave her the following exercise to try.

I told her to come around the short side of the school on the right rein, then after the short side, to ride diagonally across the school in a right leg-yield position (see pp.20–21). In this exercise you must feel what's happening in the leg yield: the horse is bent around your left leg and you're pushing him out into the outside (right) hand. That's the feeling you should have when you are riding your corners in tests. Think of leg yielding him into the corner slightly, so you ride your corners deeper. If he plops on to the forehand around the corners, lift your inside hand up and slightly against the neck, to soften him again.

Leg yielding to the right with Judi's left leg pushing into the right rein

Arnie pushes off his inside hindleg into the extended trot

I suggested to Judi that next time as she came out of the corner, she should ask for extended trot and see what happens.

Arnie showed some good extended trot strides and I was pleased to see that he really pushed off his inside hindleg as he came out of the corner.

Flying changes

Arnie's tendency to be a bit lazy with his hindlegs was also affecting his flying changes. 'He offers clean changes most of the time,' said Judi, 'but I feel he could put more effort in and show a bit more expression.'

I suggested we take a look at them, and asked her to start by riding one change across the diagonal, and after that we could look at the tempi changes.

Arnie's first change was late behind, which indicated that he wasn't engaged or on the rider's aids enough. I told Judi to ride another change, and try to get more bounce in the canter beforehand. She was a bit late to change her leg aids over, too.

Arnie's next change was better, so I asked Judi to do some four-time tempi changes down the long side. When she had

---

RIDING CHANGES

When riding a flying change, the rider must stay straight and not throw their weight over to one side. A half-halt is usually given as a preparation for the change, and then the rider's previous outside leg goes forwards. Then they ask for the change by putting the 'new' outside leg back. Their 'new' inside seatbone should lighten slightly to allow the horse's inside hindleg to step through in the change.

---

done so I laughed and admitted they weren't the best tempi changes I had ever seen. They were a bit like a chocolate assortment box – every one of them different! I told her to try again, using half-halts to get his attention, and to give him more warning with her legs.

With more preparation and more leg to create energy, Arnie's tempi changes had more lift. I told her to let him stretch.

Arnie is late changing legs behind

Judi gives him more warning and he responds with a good clean change

Long and low

In between these exercises I made sure Judi allowed Arnie to stretch, just as she would at home. For this, you must remember that the hand position should be quite different when you're riding a horse 'up' compared to when you're stretching him. For stretched work, make sure the hand is carried low and a little wider. This transfers the rein pressure on to the bars of the mouth and encourages the head and neck to lower. For a higher head carriage, the hands should be carried above the wither and more together.

Judi allows Arnie to stretch, which enables him to release his muscles and have a break as a reward for his hard work

> ## JUDI'S CONCLUSION
>
> 'I thoroughly enjoyed my lesson with Carl and found it extremely helpful, particularly the work we did towards achieving a good collected canter. At times I felt we were cantering on the spot.
>
> 'Arnie felt much more up in front, and the canter pirouette then felt achievable. We still have a fair way to go, but we're now getting sixes for our canter pirouettes, not threes and fours.
>
> 'Carl made it all seem so simple, and made me realize just how in control of each turning step I have to be, and not to just close my eyes, pray and hope we end up facing the right way!'

BEING TESTED

Most of us have limits beyond which we dare not go in our riding. This is fine if you are happy doing what you've always done, but what if you have a secret desire to be challenged?

Read 'Being tested' to learn how you can get more out of your riding. This section is devoted to working on your dressage performance, both practically and mentally. The first pages will help you to learn more about your abilities and face up to your fears. Well-known NLP (neuro-linguistic programming) practitioner Wendy Jago gets to the heart of all the problems you are likely to be facing, and gives you alternative ways of looking at them. She also describes ways of coping with your apprehensions, so that you really can do more – should you wish. Later on, several brave riding students ride a series of dressage tests and are marked on their performance. With the help of dressage judge Judy Harvey and rider Carl Hester they work on their technique, and proof of their success is revealed in the retest, when they are judged again. While dressage competitions are not the only reason to have a well-schooled and obedient horse, they can be invaluable in providing incentives for you to improve your relationship with your horse.

Move on up – Wendy Jago

Aim To find the courage to improve your achievements in dressage

Are you nervous about having a go at a Novice test, even though your trainer says you could do it easily? Perhaps you've done lots of Novice tests – even got some points – but somehow Elementary seems beyond you? If you're saying 'yes' to either of these questions, you're not alone. For some people it's confidence, for others, it's not knowing what's wanted at the new level. Perhaps you can do the movements, but then cannot string them all together. Some riders also worry that other competitors will be thinking they're not good enough. Why put yourself through it? Why not just go and do a Prelim test again…?

These are all obstacles to going up a level, and you need to dismantle them to move on. Over the next few pages I'm going to work with you so that you:

- know what's involved in going for that next level;
- understand what you need to do to help both you and your horse progress;
- discover how you could make it a natural – perhaps even enjoyable – process, instead of one that causes you and your horse anxiety, and involves joyless drilling, or the kind of marks that make you despair and convince yourself it's better to be an unchallenged non-competitor.

THE HORSES AND RIDERS

Lauren Sapstead rides *The Full Monty*, a former show-jumper; she is now concentrating on dressage with him. He is able to do higher level movements, however he tends to anticipate (for example, he offers flying changes instead of simple ones).

Annie Rowland rides *Red*, a talented Trakehner. He is spooky, especially at events, so Annie rarely goes beyond Preliminary level.

Shane Petkovic and *Ted* have been successful eventing, but Ted dislikes dressage and Shane is inhibited by self-consciousness and self-criticism.

Dressage can be fun, especially if you include plenty of variety in your training and don't keep on at any one thing

Where are you now?

I like to think of the skills and movements required for each dressage level as its *vocabulary*. So when you are considering moving up a level you need to begin by asking yourself if you and your horse have the vocabulary you need. In practice this means checking that you have the full vocabulary of the level you're currently working at, and making sure that you acquire what you need for the next level *before* you have a go. That way, you can relax and enjoy yourselves much more – and do better!

Why check out your current level? Because it's possible to compete – even regularly – at a particular level *without* having all the vocabulary. For example, when I judge Prelim classes, I see lots of horses go through a corner or make a 20m circle without actually bending to the inside. When a horse bends around the rider's inside leg, he can balance better and stay more upright, as his inside hindleg can work more efficiently to carry weight and deliver power. Even if you get away without much bend and still do the patterns, when you go up to Novice level you won't have enough balance, engagement or power for the movements. Your riding will lack fluency.

Check the vocabulary required for each level, outlined in 'Four levels of dressage' (pp.108–109). Start with your current level; check the previous levels, too. Don't look for short cuts: in the same way that you would struggle to have a sophisticated conversation in another language without knowing its basic grammar, you must have a solid foundation to do well in dressage. To increase your dressage vocabulary you need to know and be guided by the basics of athletic development, rather than just trying to ride all the movements. If you have the basics in place, the movements will come relatively easily. If, say, you find it hard to do leg yield, or you can't get your horse to back up willingly and straight, ask yourself, your trainer or a knowledgeable friend, what the steps are that make up leg yield or reinback – and work on them, rather than drilling away at more of the same. You can do this virtually anywhere! For example, when your horse is responsive to the leg, when you can control his shoulder, when he steps under willingly and takes his own weight, not only leg yields but all of the lateral movements will be much easier. Doing some of your riding with a light seat can help your horse to soften through his back and balance himself naturally, whether it is in the school or while out hacking.

Here I am helping Lauren to perfect her technique – there are no short cuts to being proficient at dressage

FOUR LEVELS OF DRESSAGE

The notes here will tell you what is assumed about the horse's level of athleticism and obedience at each level, and what new movements are required.

Preliminary

- The horse needs to be straight when you are riding straight lines, and curved when he is going through the corners and on circles.
- Circles are 20m in lower tests, 10m and 15m in some higher ones. Clear inside bend is needed, and an upright, not 'leaning', horse.
- Loops from the corner markers back to the track are 5m, requiring a degree of balance, but they start after the corner, which helps set up bend and engagement.
- Transitions are usually asked for between two markers – what's wanted is obedience and smoothness, not pinpoint accuracy.

Novice

- There are more frequent changes of bend, such as in serpentines, to demonstrate balance and lateral flexibility.
- Variety is required within the paces – for example, some medium strides – to step under and engage, to lift and stretch and then collect again (many riders don't ask for a transition back and miss out on an extra mark).
- Mini-transitions – such as trot, two to four steps in walk, then resume trot – to demonstrate obedience and balance.
- Reinback to show willingness to step back positively and straight when asked, without yanking or ducking or dragging the rider about.
- Loops in from the track and back are used to show the ability to bend the spine in both directions, and to use each hindleg in turn to create and maintain energy through the changes of direction.
- Sometimes there are four-loop serpentines, requiring much the same hindleg action but also demanding relatively rapid alternation of straightness and bending.
- Giving (releasing) and re-taking the rein shows whether the horse is carrying himself, or is being held up by the rider; also if the horse hollows on release, it reveals an over-reliance on the reins.
- Change of canter lead through trot demonstrates responsiveness to aiding, degree of balance and connection to the bit.
- 10m circles in trot require balance, bend and also engagement of the inside hindleg.
- Deeper loops (10m) in from, and back to, the track require balance and bend as above, plus lateral flexibility.
- A few counter-canter steps, such as on return to the track, requiring obedience to the aids and greater self-carriage.

Red is curving nicely on the turn, but he is 'falling in' slightly due to a loss of balance

Carl Hester shows how to give (in give and retake) the rein

Elementary

- Medium trot and canter is required for the whole of the long side. This calls for sustained engagement and a lighter forehand, as well as obedient transitions.
- Halt-to-trot, and walk-to-canter transitions. These both need more energy and responsiveness to the leg.
- Loops from the track on the long side in canter, requiring greater balance as well as more flexibility.
- 15m canter circles and 8m trot voltes, requirements as above.
- Some longer movements in counter canter, requirements as above.
- Five-loop serpentines, as above.
- Leg yields, requiring engagement of the inside hindleg and rider control of the outside shoulder to prevent falling sideways.
- Simple changes, requiring balance, obedience and a degree of collection into downward transitions, as well as engagement for upward ones.
- Shoulder-in. The horse needs to engage his inside hindleg to carry his weight. The rider has to manage a degree of bend and control the horse's shoulder to prevent it falling out, while at the same time using their leg to create enough energy and support for the horse to prevent it falling in.
- A degree of collection in trot and canter is asked for.
- Medium canter on a circle – requires a more active inside hindleg.
- Quarter pirouette requires the horse to take his weight back and lighten his shoulder, while at the same time maintaining a true and purposeful walk rhythm.

Shoulder-in is required in elementary dressage tests

Medium

- Half-pass and travers – both need the inside hind to actively carry the horse forwards and sideways while keeping the bend through his body.
- Extensions in trot and canter require the quarters to lower and propel the horse upwards as well as forwards, with a light shoulder and good self-carriage.
- Entry in canter, canter to halt, and in some tests, reinback to canter all require a light forehand and well engaged hindquarters, with the horse able to both 'sit' and 'lift' when he is asked.

To carry himself forwards and sideways in half-pass the horse must have an active inside hindleg, which is encouraged by the rider's inside leg

Make learning fun

So now you are more clear about what you need and what you don't need for each test. If you haven't got the vocabulary required, what should you do? I've already said that there are no short cuts, but there are plenty of ways to make the learning process easier. Dressage should be fun. And it can be. Here are some ideas to try in the school and/or out hacking:

• Ask for a specific canter lead from a balanced walk or an energetic trot on a hack, rather than just kicking and taking the lead your horse offers. If you let him decide out hacking, you make it harder for you to ask, and for him to answer, when you want a particular lead in the school.

• Show him that there's more than one trot and canter so he gets used to lengthening and shortening.

• Elasticize the trot on the circle, making transitions between working and medium. Doing this will make it second nature, and leave you free to think about more taxing things.

• Get him listening to your legs. I taught a young horse to do this by asking her to zigzag across a track between hedges. We also practised circles in the corners of fields.

• Ask for the best transitions you can. Prepare by thinking of what you want, then warn your horse with a shift of balance or a half-halt. That way, he'll find it easier. For downward transitions, prepare two or three strides in advance to give him time. For upward ones, half-halt to get his hindlegs under so they give a thrust.

• Try combining dressage movements and hacking out. Try trot (or walk) to canter to medium trot, then collect to turn that corner. Think working to medium to working on a circle – even in a field. Include shoulder-in as part of a pattern on a circle, with some shoulder-out or travers, and straightening. Find ways to make it natural and easy.

• Change the frame you're asking for to avoid sore muscles – his and yours! Think sitting and rising. If you're not used to sitting, do a little, often, so you don't stiffen up and bounce about in the saddle. If you mostly sit, play with standing so he can swing through his back.

• Don't keep on at any one thing. Put a pole or two in the arena, and do a couple of jumps when you're schooling.

Shane discovers standing trot, which gives Ted's back a bit of a rest

Do light-seat or standing trot and canter as a reward after working collected. Start or end your schooling session with a brief hack or some loose schooling.

• Throughout, give your horse a chance to stretch as a reward and a relief. A good athlete is supple and relaxed in mind and body – toned and not tensed. If you can set up the physical side of your training like this, you and your horse stand a really good chance of going up the levels without giving up, and of enjoying a growing partnership in athleticism. You should enjoy using your bodies together.

Vary your school work. Lauren and Monty do some rising trot across the arena

Annie rewards Red with a nice stretch at the end of the session

Getting strategic – Wendy Jago

Aim To find strategies to achieve your dressage competition ambitions

THE HORSES AND RIDERS

Shane Petkovic and *Ted*
Annie Rowland and *Red*
Lauren Sapstead and *The Full Monty*

Now you need to know how to plan an effective campaign to move up a level. Being strategic is about becoming more influential, and you can develop strategies to progress in any area of your life, including your riding. If you put the strategies suggested here into action, you'll do better in competition and feel more in control. You will also improve your riding and your horse's training.

Make sensible choices

As a judge, I'm struck by how many marks riders seem to throw away. I think this is often due to anxiety to get through the patterns, causing more fundamental things to go out the window! If you develop yourself and your horse progressively, you'll find your mind is freer to think strategically, which means two things:

1. Preparing in advance.
2. Responding effectively in the situation itself.

If you and your horse have the right vocabulary for your new dressage level, and you're prepared, you'll have more attention available in a test. This is why professionals usually compete at a level below the work they're doing at home – they're asking their horses to work within their 'comfort zone'. If something unexpected happens, they may slip momentarily into their 'stretch zone' but are less likely to go into their 'panic zone'. Stretch means you can respond and even achieve more than you'd thought. Panic means a bad experience and even anxiety for both of you. You don't want to go there.

Ask yourself whether you will be in your comfort zone:

- Is your horse attentive, balanced and flexible enough for what's being asked of him?
- Is he familiar enough with any special movements?
- Do you trust each other enough in a different situation?

If you answer 'no' to any of these, go back to playful but purposeful schooling until your answer is 'yes'. Remember: tests benchmark how far your training has come – they're not for new learning! Judges are there to tell you how it was on the day. Most judges like to praise, and feel sad if they have to tell people they are lacking in the basics.

SOME BASICS

- Prepare your transitions so that your horse is forewarned and balanced.
- Draw the shapes with your own and your horse's bodies to show straightness and bend.
- Rebalance before any transition or new movement.
- Be aware that you can influence your horse through changing your posture.

Shane bravely demonstrates how a rider with a curled posture produces a collapsed horse…

…then shows how a rider with a straight posture produces a more balanced, collected horse

Choose the right test

Tests come in groups for the different levels, but they aren't all asking for the same things. Apart from the obvious differences between the lower numbered ones (easier) and the higher numbered ones (more difficult), tests on the same level can require different things. Once you've worked out what a particular test calls for, you can enter the ones you and your horse find easier, and avoid those you will find harder until you've developed your skills more.

Some tests call for lots of transitions, within and between the paces, which need good engagement and balance and a readiness to listen and respond quickly to the aids. Some call for lots of changes of bend, which demand suppleness through the back. Some call for the horse to carry himself sideways and forwards at the same time (lateral work).

Imagine the test as a whole. What's the overall emphasis? Can you and your horse produce what is wanted? There's nothing wrong with choosing a test that shows you to the best advantage!

Make arena size a reason to choose which tests to enter for. If you have a big gangly youngster, he'll balance himself more easily in a large arena where the movements come less thick and fast – and there are a few long arena tests at the lower levels. With a pony, avoid long arenas as much as you can – he'll have to put in proportionately more effort than a bigger horse

and may run out of steam. If you have a stocky cob, make the most of tests that ask for 'some lengthening' rather than lengthening for the whole diagonal or long side, as cobs often find it hard to lift and lengthen. And make the most of corners to rebalance your horse and get his hocks under him before lengthening so he has the best chance to show a difference.

Use competition time to benchmark the things you feel happiest with, and use training time to hone your skills and add new ones. If you compete inside your comfort zone, you will have space, attention and confidence to manage the extra demands of being at a different, perhaps busy, venue and having to perform in front of others.

> ### KNOW WHAT'S INVOLVED
>
> - Draw out your test on paper making a mini-arena rectangle for each movement. Use different colour pens for walk, trot and canter so that you can see where the transitions occur.
> - Imagine being your horse going through that sequence of movements. What do you need to be able to do?

Shane and Ted try out walk pirouette. This is an early attempt and it doesn't look pretty, but everyone has to start somewhere! Remaining calm and working through the movements slowly will pay dividends in the end

Don't dwell on problems

If things don't quite go to plan during your test, use your best skill to keep communication going with your horse. If you make a mistake, put it firmly behind you straightaway; don't listen to that critical inner voice telling you how stupid or useless you are, and instead focus on making the movements that follow as good as you possibly can. After all, your horse doesn't have any idea that you forgot the test – if you stop communicating with him just because you're having words with yourself, then he will start to lose confidence because he feels that you've abandoned him, and as a result you may have more problems.

If your horse becomes spooky during a test, try your best to reassure him, but also remember to ride him firmly forwards to help re-establish his confidence and regain his attention. If necessary, turn his head slightly away from whatever made him spook – much better to lose a mark for going shoulder-fore or even shoulder-in than lose two or three marks for spooking a second time! If you forget the test and go wrong, remember that you can bring in a commander, even once the test is under way. Don't be too proud to ask a friend to come and help you if you think that you might go wrong again.

Practise best practice

Rehearse yourself more than you rehearse your horse. A trained horse has learnt to anticipate: certain aids mean canter, others mean trot, or halt, for example. What you don't want is for him to get the test set in his mind. Once horses start to learn flying changes, for example, it can be hard to get a simple change or to stay in counter canter. Practise all the movements, and transitions of course, as part of your everyday riding. And make sure you run through the test as a whole in your head and even on your feet, but don't drill your horse on the test, or he'll pay more attention to the pattern than to what you're asking him for on the day. Hacking can be a real help. Build in some dressage movements when you're out on the fields and tracks and it will help your horse to think of them as requests rather than routines. My friend Gary gets his advanced horses doing their tempi changes like this. As part of a free and forward canter, changes can feel like unforced, joyous skipping!

Make dressage part of your regular work, when riding out, rather than something you only do when you're preparing for a competition. The foundation of dressage is the foundation of all good riding – rhythm, relaxation, contact, impulsion, straightness and collection. You can develop these as well when you are jumping and hacking as you can in the school.

By riding forwards positively Annie reassures Red that there is nothing to be worried about

Think of your dressage position and your horse's outline as a set of 'clothing' that truly fits and belongs to you. You can choose to wear it, or to put on other sets of clothing that you own (such as hacking, or jumping), but you know that it fits and suits you because you wear it regularly. If you don't, then sitting correctly and working through into an outline will pinch like stilletos that give you blisters, or a jacket that feels so formal, and just 'not me'.

It is important to remember that different rider postures suit different situations and achieve different effects. If you want to compete at dressage, you have to ensure that you look like someone who does it naturally and easily – not just because it looks good, but also because it does the job, achieving the way of going that you want from your horse at that time.

Shane and Ted enjoy some flatwork practise – working together calmly and efficiently

GETTING EXPERIENCE

Look for unaffiliated competitions that encourage you to 'have a go' at higher levels. Some venues put on mixed level shows. In these, a single class might include named Novice, Elementary and Medium tests, allowing the rider to choose which they want to do. The prizes go to the highest scorers in a class regardless of the level – thus a good novice might do better than a horse trying medium for the first time – or vice versa.

Some clubs go one step further and give rosettes for all horses that get certain scores (such as above 60% or 65%) without having placings. This allows you and your horse to flex your competition muscles and get feedback without putting yourselves publicly on the line. If you can't find classes like this, ask your riding club to put some on. Or organize one with some friends. Be inventive!

Gaining extra marks

In most tests, certain key movements easily lose or gain you marks, so they're well worth your attention and practise:

1. **Clear transitions within the pace** – such as before and after lengthening the stride. If you show a clear difference in stride length with a crisp, upward transition and a well balanced downward one, as a judge I'd be thinking seven or better. If you don't – especially if you don't show a clear transition back – you're throwing away at least one mark.

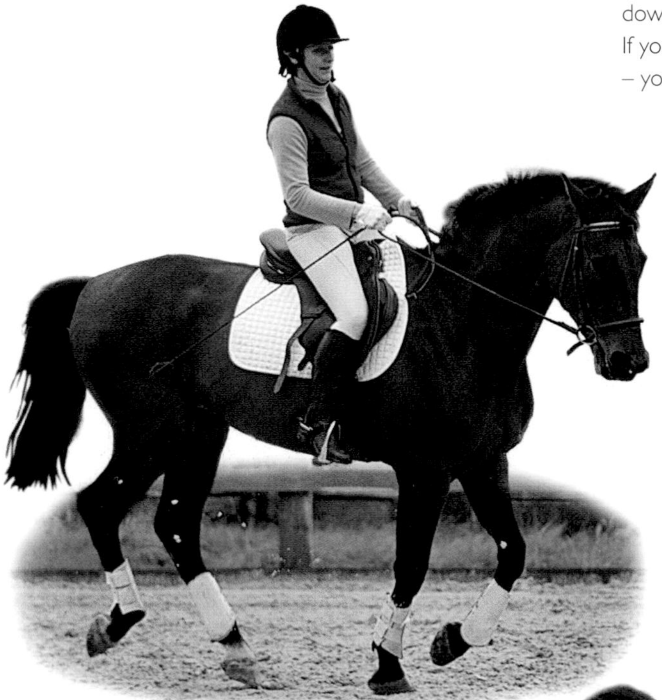

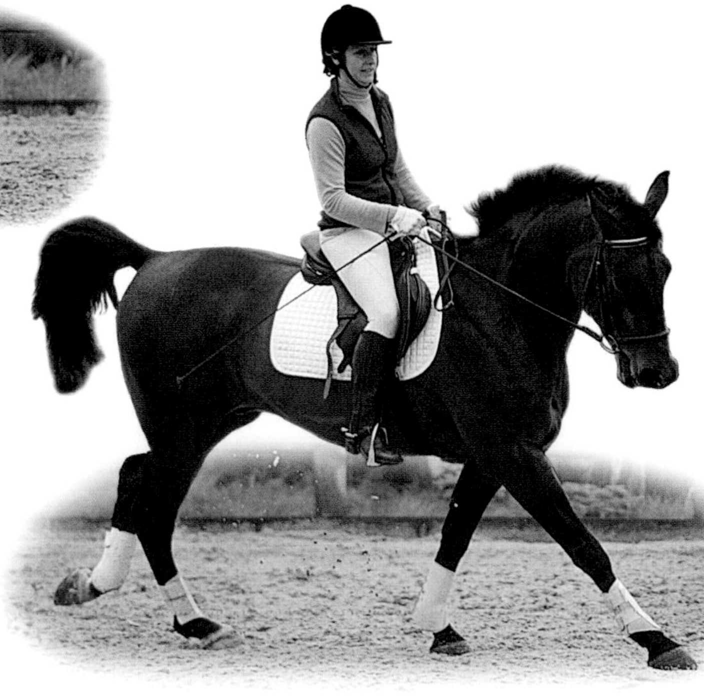

Annie and Red demonstrate a good transition from collected canter to medium canter

2. Turns on to and off the centre line

If you can ride a straight centre line that flows into a well bent corner in the same rhythm, or turns across the arena (including serpentines) clearly showing bend-straight-bend, you maximize your chances of demonstrating your horse's obedience and lateral suppleness. If you drift through the turns and there's no visible straightness parallel with the short side of the arena, you're throwing easy marks away.

3. Inside bend on turns and circles

My husband Leo often writes for me when I'm judging. He is thinking of ordering a rubber stamp that says 'needs more inside bend' because I say this so often! Why does it matter? Because it helps your horse balance and carry himself better, and because it is, in itself, a way of developing and showing his suppleness through the back.

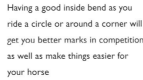

Having a good inside bend as you ride a circle or around a corner will get you better marks in competition as well as make things easier for your horse

4. Well prepared downward transitions

If you warn your horse with a rebalancing half-halt or two before asking for a downward transition, he has the chance to step under with his hindlegs and carry himself forwards into the transition, rather than sliding into it with a hollow back, or falling on to his nose with his hindlegs all splayed out behind (the latter often makes for an unbalanced, crooked or restless halt). Good preparation is kinder to your horse, helps him develop his self-carriage, and should contribute towards improving your rider mark!

THE SECRETS OF HALF-HALT – TINA SEDERHOLM, DAISY DICK, JAMES FISHER

What is a half-halt and how do you do it? Three well known equestrians give their opinions.

Tina Sederholm

Tina is a best-selling author and is rapidly becoming one of the most respected trainers of our time.

A half-halt is a change you make in the horse's way of going to improve his balance (that is, to shift bodyweight from his forehand to his hindquarters). The result is a gathering of power, because the horse increases the elevation in his stride, and his rhythm improves. This makes it easier for him to carry out whatever you want to do next. Think of it as a bit like when you make a smooth downward gear change in a car before a steep hill. The car feels powerful and much more able to handle the gradient, and yet more under your control.

Half-halts are one of the rider's most useful tools. Horses are built for speed and so naturally tend to have their centre of gravity quite far forward. When we want them to execute movements in a confined area, or in a controlled way, they need to be able to transfer their centre of gravity back; in other words, to take more weight on their hindquarters than their forehand. A half-halt works in two ways: it sets up the horse for the next movement by mentally alerting him that something is coming, and by physically preparing him to carry out the movement by transferring more weight on to his hocks. You can use them before turning through a corner, before a transition or a change of pace, and before any movement such as a circle or a sideways movement.

The better balanced he is, the more a horse is capable of maintaining weight on his hindquarters, so the less you need half-halts before simple movements like turns and circles.

A half-halt shifts the horse's weight and power to the hindquarters

Engage the top half of your body, close and raise your hands slightly, then close your legs firmly

• Riding a half-halt

Half-halts range from a light touch on the reins to a proper classical half-halt, the most advanced version being piaffe. A classical half-halt involves the rider starting the action by becoming more vertical with their top body, contracting their stomach muscles and engaging their back. A half second or so later, they close the hand, perhaps raising it slightly if necessary, and a half second or so after that, close their legs around the horse in a hugging fashion. It is important that the rider gets the order of the aids correct – body, hand, leg.

Many riders make the mistake of using the hand first, which causes the horse to lean into the half-halt, putting more weight on the front end – the opposite effect from the one intended. It takes lots of practice to get the timing perfect, so with a young horse or rider, I tend to teach them to respond to the seat and hand aids first. Once the rider is consistently carrying out the first two aids in the correct order, they can then add the hugging leg, so the horse is supported in bending his hindlegs more.

Daisy Dick
Dasiy won Blenheim International Horse Trials in 2006.

In jumping, half-halts are vital for balance and control on turns between fences, and in front of fences. They help to build up controlled energy without losing the front end, are vital for balance and to be able to ride with accuracy, and to control the horse's pace.

The half-halt is obtained using a rein aid, varying in strength and duration depending on the training of the horse, with a simultaneous increase in pressure from the leg. As the horse shortens and is felt to step under himself, there is an obvious softening of the hand as the horse is rewarded for his response and a feeling of moving forwards. Half-halts need to be applied as little or as often as necessary for the horse to learn to respond to a light touch. Sometimes it is helpful with a young horse to use a little voice in training – a gentle 'whoa' should help him understand what you are asking for.

James Fisher
James has been a regular member of the British show jumping squad for more than 20 years and has represented Great Britain on 25 Nations Cup team competitions.

Basically, a half-halt is a momentary pause or change of speed, to help prepare a horse for whatever instruction or movement is coming next. It's a way of telling a horse to shift his weight back to his hindquarters.

A half-halt is a useful tool for alerting the horse that something is about to happen, be it an upward or downward transition – say, for a trot-to-canter transition, a walk-to-canter transition or a change of direction – it's also a good building block for a change of leg. If you think about doing a half-halt every time you go into canter, for example, it should encourage your horse to 'jump' into canter, rather than 'flatten' and run into it.

In show-jumping, riders do it a lot, almost without noticing – it's practically a reflex action. Simply put on your inside leg and 'squeeze' the outside rein – doing this is almost teaching the horse to brace himself and shorten to the outside rein. You shorten and he will shorten!

Excuses, excuses, excuses – Wendy Jago

Aim To overcome your fears, and do what you want to do

THE HORSES AND RIDERS

Shane Petkovic and *Ted*

Annie Rowland and *Red*

Lauren Sapstead and *The Full Monty*

MIND CONTROL

Your horse can read your mind, and he will reflect what he reads in the way he behaves:

- Anxious rider – tense horse
- Driven rider – stiff horse
- Ambitious rider – lonely horse

Think about these for a moment. They are typical scenarios even among people who really care, meaning they achieve the very opposite of what they want. I'm assuming that you love your horse and enjoy being with him. Why not feel like that in competition, too?

'If something's worth doing, it's worth doing badly,' said Oscar Wilde. In other words, where something is worthwhile, have a go at it, even if you know you can't yet do it well. Get involved. Learn. How much would it change how you think about competition if you approached it in this light? And how much would it affect your horse? When I'm judging, I often see tense riders and miserable horses, delivering a performance that I'm sure is nowhere near as good as they can produce at home. Horses and riders I've seen producing high quality work in training can also look disappointing in competition. I'm convinced that one reason for this is that the rider is allowing unhelpful thoughts to run through her head while she competes – thoughts that she never entertains when she's at home. When she thinks of moving up a level, it gets even worse.

Put it into perspective

Here are eight attitudes towards tests and performance, and some advice on how to break them. Think of them as tactics for getting your attitudes, beliefs and expectations into as good a shape as possible for moving up a dressage level. Mental fitness can be schooled and built, just like physical fitness. I want to begin by dismantling some fantasies (misconceptions) that often lie behind performance anxiety. (You can substitute jumping or hacking out for 'dressage' in many of them.)

1. If I'm serious about dressage, I really ought to go out and compete

I have had sad letters from committed riders who felt they were pressurized to compete by their friends, families or trainers, even though they didn't want to. Not everyone is competitive, and some people prefer schooling and training at home. So I want to say right away that *it's your choice* whether you compete or not. In *Dressage Principles Illuminated* Charles de Kunffy says: '…competition never proved to have any merit in ranking true equestrian knowledge. Some of the greatest riders in the world do not compete … riding skills, scholarship and personal attributes, not competition scores, should matter in ranking riders.'

Is competing on *your* agenda – or someone else's? Your first and most important test may be in finding the courage – and the words – to tell them that their agenda is not for you.

You do not have to compete to ride well and have a responsive, well trained horse – Wendy Jago rides Ollie, owned by Nikki Green

2. Dressage tests are a form of examination

For many people the idea of 'tests' brings up unhappy or even traumatic memories of school. Instead, try thinking of a test as a kind of snapshot of your riding partnership at a specific moment. If you look through those hundreds of riding photos you've probably got, each one of them is an accurate record of a split second, yet I'm sure many of them don't really reveal what your riding is like overall. You pick out the best ones to frame, and you throw away the worst – both can also surprise you. All are 'true' for that split second, but may not reflect your riding as a whole.

What happens if you think of a test, and the 'snapshot' the test sheet gives you, like this? By being 'natural' in front of the judge's camera-like eyes, you and your horse will stay more relaxed and focused on what you're doing.

You and your horse can have plenty of fun practising all your dressage moves. Just enjoy the processes of learning and improving

Think of a test as a snapshot of your riding
– you are not stuck at this place in time

3. Dressage is different from ordinary riding

Only if you make it so! Good flatwork is the foundation of all the disciplines because it helps develop not only your shared athleticism, but also your skills in communicating with each other. It hones your partnership and makes everything you do with your horse safer, less taxing on muscles and joints – and more fun!

If you think of dressage as something different, your horse will pick up on this. So the more that you make use of your everyday riding to practise and polish your aiding, and to fine-tune his responses, the less difference there will be. One of my best 'dressage moments' was picking sloes on a bridleway from the back of our horse Lolly. He gave me the height I needed, and because of our shared dressage vocabulary, he was able to move, and stand patiently, where I wanted and when I wanted, for a good half hour – then carry the heavy bag of sloes home on his withers!

As for competition … think of it as 'schooling away from home'. Then warm-up becomes like warm-up at home, and the test itself becomes the workout part of your session instead of something strange and terrifying.

4. Dressage tests involve being judged

Most of us have some trouble with the idea of being judged because it can make us feel inferior. Plus, because we put so much of ourselves into our riding, when someone criticizes our performance it can feel like it's a personal criticism of us or our equine friend, so a judge's remarks seem like a verdict on our character, not a comment on our skill. But remember, there doesn't have to be quite so much at stake – just don't allow there to be.

5. Doing a test is about winning or losing

Riding a test can bring great pleasure – provided you're the winner or among the placings. But if you compete, and especially if you choose to attempt the next level up, it is best to find other ways of thinking about winning or losing. You want to feel you have achieved something, whatever your mark, and you and your horse need to stay happy and confident in your work if you are to keep going.

Try setting up some different goals for yourself – ones that you could potentially achieve, whoever else is out there, and whether or not you 'do well'. Set your sights on things such as having a good time, staying in the ring, staying focused, doing as well as last time or even better, learning to cope with the unexpected, keeping your horse straighter, or more bent, lighter, or more attentive… the list of worthwhile aims is limitless.

Think of your dressage test as schooling away from home

Even fantastic dressage riders, such as Carl Hester, started their competition career at the bottom, as did your dressage judges. Here Carl rides half-pass on Madonna

6. If I try a higher level, I'll be up against people who have more skills and better horses, so I'm bound to feel inadequate and do badly

Nip this one firmly in the bud by thinking of the test as an experiment, a stretch, a workout, a learning opportunity. Of course there will be riders and horses there who can work easily at this level. Some of them may have been competing at this level for a while (unaffiliated, you could do it pretty indefinitely). They may be putting off going up to their next level, just as you have been.

From years of working as a therapist and coach, I know that the world is full of able, confident-looking people who inside feel scared, self-critical, and as though they have no right to be where they are. You can remind yourself of this as they appear to carve you up in the warm-up arena – or, more productively, allow them and yourself to be human, make mistakes, and learn from them. This is the point of getting into the stretch zone, because you don't learn in your comfort zone.

7. If I get low marks I shall feel really bad about myself

If this is what you're expecting, of course you will. You may have to make a real effort, but set yourself up before the competition to translate any negative comments into positive suggestions. For example, 'not enough bend' could become 'practise bending'; 'not in front of the leg' becomes 'do more of those concertina exercises', 'make sure I get my horse going forward every time', and 'more spiralling in and out in a good working trot'.

Judges are not supposed to give a riding lesson, and they are working against time when judging. This sometimes means that their comments sound negative. Also, some lower-listed judges can be so anxious about their ability to spot what's wrong that they are less ready to praise. You could always buttonhole your judge afterwards and ask her how to achieve what she thinks you lack.

8. My horse behaves differently when we're at shows

Now isn't that a surprise? His surroundings are different, and he probably knows from your preparations beforehand that he's going to a party. Some horses, like people, find parties exciting – others dread them.

Before you even think of competing, work on building up the kind of partnership that means you listen to each other, whatever else is going on. There are so many everyday opportunities for this: out hacking when kids are in the school playground, when a pheasant shoots out of the hedge, in the arena when the other owner's dogs run in and out or put up a rabbit in the next field, when someone starts cantering just near you, when the local farmer takes a pot-shot at a rabbit, in the yard when someone moves the hose, and so on.

If you have trained yourself to take your horse positively through experiences like this, the unexpected things that happen in competitions won't faze you nearly so much. You'll be able to stay focused when the advertising banners flap, when a horse kicks the side of its lorry or clatters down the ramp, even when the resident peacock flies into the arena (yes, this really happened!).

I've seen all these, when judging; for some horses and riders they were a disaster, but for others they were just something else to be calmly registered, quickly coped with or even virtually ignored while they simply got on with the job in hand.

A good strategy can be to take your horse to a show – and not compete. Walk him around, let him see what it's like, give him time to acclimatize. The more often he goes out in a calm frame of mind the easier you will both find it.

OVERCOMING YOUR FEARS

- Are any of these eight fantasies getting in your way? Dismantle the fantasy in your mind and put more realistic thoughts in its place!
- Look at the situation from different perspectives. How might it seem to your horse? To your friends and family? And to the judge? They would all much prefer that you had a good time and were relaxed and able to work at your best.
- Identify problem areas, and work to overcome them. Someone asked me how to deal with her fear of falling off when jumping. I asked if she had ever fallen off, and she said 'No' – a light-bulb moment!

Riding your horse through spooks in the school prepares you for scary competition arenas

Calmness in horse and rider

- Competing doesn't have to be an unseen test. Watch other people, look at their marks, ask yourself how you would judge them. Offer to write for judges – you will learn a lot about what they are looking for. Make the most of your teacher, your friends, books and videos, pair up with a friend and help each other in training and on the day.

- Remember the good times and the good work, and go over them in your mind as many times as it takes to help build your confidence. Think about every situation you have shared with your horse, not just the competition ones (perhaps these least of all!) What was your best walk, your best canter, your best circle? You want to know in your mind's eye just what it looked like (from inside and outside); to feel again in your mind how it felt then in your muscles and your bones; and you need to hear the encouragement of people who care about you, and to talk positively to yourself.

- If you find that you keep running disaster scenarios through your mind, work on changing the endings and make them turn out positively. People often instinctively stop their internal disaster movies at the most frightening moment, which reinforces the effect! Work out how to get a better ending, and then play and replay it in your mind until it overwrites the old ending.

You and your horse are a partnership, and this remains the most important thing – no matter what happens in the competition arena

Remember all the good work that you have done with your horse

The tests

Over the next few pages dressage rider and trainer Carl Hester and dressage judge Judy Harvey take some willing volunteers through the experience of a dressage test. In a carefully worked out series of sessions, the pair observed several horse and rider partnerships doing dressage tests, which they were marked on as if they were taking part in real tests. Judy and Carl then had a chat with each rider to highlight their strengths and areas for improvement. After this, Carl gave each horse and rider a 20–30 minute lesson to improve those areas that he and Judy had picked up on. The horse and rider then rode the test again after a short break, and their performance was assessed.

Among the most satisfying things about riding flatwork is being at one with your horse

Get active – Carl Hester and Judy Harvey

Aim To assess a horse and rider through Novice Test 36 and help them to improve their score

> ### HORSE AND RIDER
> *Simon Burton* is 18 years old and has competed in Pony Club dressage, show jumping and cross-country. He prefers dressage, and has competed successfully at unaffiliated Preliminary and Novice level; last year he qualified to compete in the Pony Club dressage championships at Sansaw.
>
> *Just Jaz* is a coloured 15.2hh warmblood mare. She is seven years old, and Simon has owned her since just after she was backed three years ago.

The first test – Judy Harvey

Under test conditions, Simon and Jaz rode an accurate test, but incurred deductions on various movements.

Their entry up the centre line was nice and straight, but after the halt, Jaz was reluctant to resume the trot. In their 10m circles and serpentine movements, I felt that although Jaz had a good rhythm, she was a little on the forehand, with too much neck bend.

The pair showed no real lengthening in the medium trot strides the first time, as Jaz's trot just quickened – however, their second attempt later in the test was better. In the medium canter, again there was little difference shown between working and medium canter on the right rein, so the marks were low; but they improved their marks on the left rein, albeit I felt the canter needed to be more 'uphill'.

The reinback caused the pair a problem. This is one of the more demanding Novice tests, and reinback was a movement that Simon and Jaz had not had previous experience of. Then on the final trot half circle to the centre line, Jaz came behind the vertical and the halt was not square.

The collective marks summarized Simon and Jaz's performance, in that I gave them sixes for paces, submission and rider's position, but only five for impulsion.

My comments were as follows: 'Correct paces, but the horse needs to be straighter and more engaged.' Their total percentage was 58.46%.

Too much bend makes Jaz hollow and she falls out through the shoulder

Jaz tends not to be straight through her turns

Feedback

After Simon's test, Carl and I discussed it with him. Describing their performance, I said that Jaz maintained a good rhythm, but it was a bit slow. She is quite sluggish and gives minimum effort, which was highlighted in her first attempt at lengthened strides. Her second was better and showed promise – so we know she can do it!

I also told him that he tended to have too much bend in her neck, so she falls out and falls on the forehand. I observed that her reinback was the weakest thing, but then she hadn't done this before so that was to be expected.

Carl added: "You need energy in your test. Rhythm is important, but with energy! You could have used the time working in around the arena to your advantage, but you just trotted around slowly. To get her in front of your leg, do some transitions, start, stop, canter – energize her before going into the arena."

The lesson – Carl Hester

Creating energy

At the beginning of our lesson, I asked Simon to work on creating energy in Jaz's trot. I emphasized that when he asked her to go more forwards he shouldn't need to make a big effort – she should react to light leg aids. At walk he was squeezing her constantly and she wasn't doing anything. She should walk like a racehorse with her neck out and going somewhere. At the moment she's going as slow as a snail!

I described a useful exercise for Simon to get Jaz more energized and going forwards: first 'click' her to ask her to go forwards, then if there is no response, take your legs off and give her a little kick with your heel until she canters – then walk again. Use your voice and get a reaction. So click first, then if necessary give her a little kick until she's in a powerful canter, and she's switched on. Then when you click again, she'll be ready to go.

I explained that there's no point taking up the reins when there is no energy in the horse's stride. And to encourage the horse to think forwards, when this exercise is practised, the rider needs to do it on a long rein so the horse is not restricted when she responds.

As the lesson continued, I reminded Simon from time to time to keep the trot active, and if Jaz became a bit sluggish again that he should repeat the 'forwards' exercise.

NOVICE TEST 36

Simon and Just Jaz

FIRST TEST RESULTS	
COMMENT	**MARK**
Straight entry but reluctant in take off	6/10
Quite good rhythm in trot on 10m circle but getting on the forehand	6/10
A little on the forehand during four-loop serpentine	7/10
Working trot and 10m circle left had too much neck bend	6/10
Medium trot strides showed no real lengthening, tending to quicken	5/10
Halt and reinback not really achieved, very reluctant	4/10
Medium walk had correct rhythm, but lack of willing forward movement	12/20
Working canter left	7/10
20m circle give and retake had too much neck bend and on forehand	5/10
Working canter with medium canter strides – no clear difference	5/10
Working canter and change rein	6/10
Change of leg through trot	7/10
20m circle working canter, give and retake – should give the contact more	6/10
Working canter with medium canter strides – better difference than before	6/10
Working canter and working trot	7/10
Change rein show some medium trot strides – some lengthening but needs to be more uphill	6/10
10m half circle left to X, down centre line and halt – behind vertical in half circle and not quite square in halt	5/10
Paces	12/20
Impulsion	10/20
Submission	12/20
Rider's position, seat correctness and effectiveness of aids	12/20
Comment: Correct paces but need to be straighter and more engaged	
Total score 152 = 58.4%	

Simon and Jaz perform superb, energized and lengthened trot strides

Reducing bend

The root of two key problems for Simon and Jaz was too much neck bend, which caused Jaz to become heavy on the forehand and to fall out through her shoulder.

I observed that when Simon collected up his reins to ask for trot, he only picked up his left rein and tweaked Jaz to the left, which meant she fell out through the right shoulder. I suggested he use both reins and squeeze her round the corners, and told him he should see straight down her neck and through her ears – you won't see that through a bent, crooked neck.

Simon picked this up quickly and, combined with a more active trot, they were able to make a smoother, more balanced turn. I was impressed with the pair, and said so! Now that he had two reins in contact Jaz wasn't falling out, and she had a more positive rhythm.

Smoothing turns and squaring halts

In their first test, Simon and Jaz had only received a five for their half circle on to the centre line and halt. Jaz wasn't straight through her body and therefore fell out through the shoulder on the turn, and she stepped sideways in the halt.

I explained that when you come on to the centre line, you shouldn't just turn with your inside rein, but should bring the horse's shoulders to the left using both reins. I advised Simon to support Jaz through the turn with the outside rein, and use the inside leg to create the bend – not the inside rein.

I made what I hoped were some useful suggestions for improving the halt transition, at this stage of their training: to keep control of the transition from trot to halt, take a step of walk before the halt. Likewise after the halt at the beginning of a test, take a step of walk before the trot transition.

I then suggested that Simon give Jaz a break and return to walk – but warned him not to let her return to her snail's pace, but to make her walk like they were in the paddocks at Ascot! Even having a break she should walk with positive energy.

And when Simon and Jaz produced the walk I was looking for, I told him it was only like this that he'd get Jaz fit enough for dressage work, so she had more energy. Just trotting and cantering around won't do that.

Lengthening strides and improving transitions

I wanted to help Simon and Jaz with their lengthened strides in canter, and their walk-to-canter transitions. Jaz needed to 'jump' higher in the canter, so she needed to be straight and using her hindlegs. On a circle in canter, I told Simon to bend her to the outside so she wasn't over-bending to the inside, and push her round the circle with the outside leg. Then use the inside leg to make her jump into the canter.

Simon keeps his outside rein to maintain Jaz's straightness through turns

Simon manages to get more 'jump' into Jaz's canter

Putting all that he'd learnt into practise, Simon was able to give and retake the reins successfully too! However, when I asked them to canter down the long side, I observed that although Jaz was now straighter through the neck, her quarters had swung a little to the inside of the track. To counteract this, I explained that Simon needed to bring Jaz's shoulders to the inside, but to keep her straight using his outside rein so that she didn't bend too much to the inside again.

I also asked them to do lots of transitions from trot to walk, back to trot and canter, and it was clear that Simon needed to think quicker in order to plan each transition or movement. I advised him that you need to think about keeping the horse straight with the outside rein before you trot, and plan for a turn. Don't just use your rein at the last minute – there's no excuse for falling out twice in a row! On the left rein Simon found this more difficult, because he had a naughty left hand, which persisted in creating too much neck bend. It was obviously tempting for him to pull back on it, but I told him it was a habit he'd have to get rid of.

Simon worked hard to put all this advice into practice, and it began to come together nicely. It was a lovely picture, and Jaz showed good paces and rhythm. At the time Simon was doing most of the work, but I assured him that when she learned to do the job on her own, he'd get lots of extra marks. You can't make a horse supple in a day but 'Jaz will improve if you practise at home,' I concluded.

The retest – Judy Harvey

Simon's second test certainly proved they'd got themselves together and were working more positively. He scored more highly in many movements – getting sevens instead of fives and sixes – simply because the paces and rhythm were more forwards, and they had a good outline and rhythm. Specifically, the pair showed a good difference in their lengthened strides in canter this time, and managed an eight for their give and retake the reins in canter!

I commented that they were much improved; they now needed to maintain this balance and rhythm to make their test marks more consistent. And the proof was in the points – Simon and Jaz got 64.62% for their second attempt!

Simon has transformed Jaz's lacklustre trot (right) to an impressive, active one (top), which Jaz performs in a nice round outline

The pair make an excellent turn with just the right amount of bend

Previously, Jaz's canter lacked energy and lift (above), but in their second test (top) it had more of a 'jump', and they even scored an eight!

NOVICE TEST 36

Simon and Just Jaz

RETEST RESULTS	
COMMENT	MARK
Entry and halt – quarters slightly to the right but positive energy	7/10
Good outline and rhythm in working trot on 10m circle right	7/10
Four-loop serpentine – some stiffness in turns but good rhythm	7/10
Working trot and 10m circle left – still too much neck bend	6/10
Medium trot strides – showing some difference but tending to hurry	6/10
Halt and reinback – reluctant but achieved	6/10
Change rein in medium walk – could be rounder but good steps	12/20
Working canter left	6/10
20m circle left, give and retake the reins – still too much neck bend	6/10
Working canter with medium canter strides – good difference	7/10
Working canter and change rein	7/10
Change of leg through trot – rather late	5/10
20m circle working canter, give and retake – should give the contact more	8/10
Working canter with medium canter strides – better difference than before	7/10
Working canter and working trot	7/10
Change rein and show some medium trot strides, working trot – some lengthening but needs to be more uphill	6/10
10m half-circle left to X, down centre line and halt – needs to be rounder	6/10
Paces	14/20
Impulsion	12/20
Submission	12/20
Rider's position, seat correctness and effectiveness of aids	14/20
Comment: Much better, now need to maintain balance and rhythm	
Total score 168 = 64.62%	

HOMEWORK – CARL HESTER

- Practise the 'forwards' exercise – Simon must get Jaz to think forwards and respond to light leg aids using the 'click, then kick' exercise.
- Don't over-bend – Simon should take care not to tweak Jaz with the left rein; instead he needs to keep her straighter to the outside rein and push her into the corners with his inside leg.
- Straighten the canter – Simon should turn Jaz's shoulders slightly on to the inside track on the long sides, to prevent her quarters falling in, while using the outside rein to keep her straight.

On the right track – Carl Hester and Judy Harvey

Aim To assess a horse and rider through Novice Test 36 and help them to improve their score

The first test – Judy Harvey

Once they had warmed up, Ann and Sunnie came into the arena and rode Novice 36 as if they were riding in a competition. Their test was very consistent, and they finished on a mark of 58.84%, scoring three sevens in the process! I commented on how accurately Ann rode a lot of the movements, and observed that Sunnie had nice paces. However, I felt that the horse became a bit hollow at times, and that the trot needed to be more active.

HORSE AND RIDER

Ann McCarvey has owned *Shepley High Flyer (Sunnie)* for 12 years. She enjoys dressage, fun rides, show-jumping and endurance. Sunnie is a 16-year-old, three-quarter Arab gelding. He qualified for the Preliminary regionals last year.

Ann says: 'Sunnie is quite sharp, with a sense of humour and a mind of his own. He owns an encyclopedia of evasions!'

Sunnie tilts his nose to the left on a circle

NOVICE TEST 36

Ann and Sunnie

FIRST TEST RESULTS	
COMMENT	**MARK**
Entry – nose tilting to left, hold whip in rein hand when saluting; obedient	5/10
Fairly active trot on 10m circle but needs more bend, and through corners	6/10
Could be more supple in four-loop serpentine, lost rhythm on last loop	5/10
Working trot and 10m circle left was good although balance was lost at B	7/10
Change rein and medium trot strides – showed some lengthening, but could move more from behind, unbalanced at F	6/10
Halt and reinback – rather reluctant	4/10
Change rein in medium walk was regular but could be straighter	14/20
Working canter left was a little against the hand	6/10
20m circle left, give and retake the reins – could be rounder	6/10
Working canter with medium canter strides – tending to hollow, could show more stride difference	5/10
Working canter and change rein	6/10
Change of leg through trot	7/10
20m circle right in working canter, give and retake – needs to be rounder	6/10
Working canter with medium canter strides – losing balance	6/10
Working canter and working trot	6/10
Change rein and show some medium trot strides – against hand and tending to hurry	5/10
10m half-circle left to X, down centre line and halt – overshot halt, needs to be on bit in halt	5/10
Paces	14/20
Impulsion	12/20
Submission	10/20
Rider's position, seat correctness and effectiveness of aids	12/20
Comment: Nice type of horse with good movement	
Total score 152 = 58.84%	

In the four-loop serpentine, Ann and Sunnie lost their balance slightly on the last loop, which caused the rhythm to vary. They did show some medium trot strides, although these needed to come more from behind.

Sunnie scored a seven for his lovely walk, and this mark would have been even higher if the pair had stayed straighter through the movement. Sunnie was inclined to tilt his nose to the left on the circles and down the centre lines, which reduced their marks.

Feedback

So what was Carl's verdict? 'I like Sunnie. He's a very attractive and willing horse with good, forward-going paces. I'd like to see his hindlegs stepping through from behind more, so that he is tracking up.

'Also, I'd like to work on getting the horse rounder in his outline – although that should improve once his hindlegs are more active,' he added.

The lesson – Carl Hester

Tracking up

Watching Ann and Sunnie in trot, I noticed something interesting: when you leave him alone, he tracks up, but when you try and pick him up on to a shorter contact, he stops tracking up. I advised Ann that, because he shortened his stride when she rode him on a shorter contact, she needed to ride him with a longer neck so he stretched his topline more and lifted his back; this would help him track up better. And in this more stretched position, Sunnie immediately began to track up.

Sunnie tracks up well when his trot is active (above), but he stops doing this when Ann rides him in a shorter contact (inset)

Flexing without tilting

Next I asked Ann to come on to a right-rein 20m circle, and to stay in rising trot and open her inside rein so that Sunnie flexed more to the inside. As she flexed him, I told her to give him a little kick with the inside leg to step him up into her left rein. But just as he did in the test, Sunnie brought his neck to the right when Ann flexed him, but tilted his nose out to the left.

I reassured her that I had a solution for tilty noses: if you lift your right rein up, you'll find the horse's nose comes right, too.

I had one final thing to add: I told Ann she had very still hands, which is not a bad thing, but sometimes it's okay to have a bit of movement in the stillness to help the horse stay rounder. It's a case of making your messages clearer to him.

Improving accuracy

In dressage, every combination of horse and rider will have strengths and weaknesses, but there is one thing that all riders can do to pick up extra marks, regardless of what their horse is like – and that is, be accurate.

I told Ann that when she rode her test, her 10m circles were too big. And I'd have liked to have seen her ride into the corners more, too. I told her to go large, and at every corner, to lift the inside hand slightly to get better inside bend, use the inside leg to push the horse out into the corners, and be sure to keep a contact on the outside rein so that he doesn't cut the corners.

I recommended that she rode every corner as though she were going to start a 10m circle in that corner. Corners are really important at Novice level because every movement starts from one, so you need to use the corner to set up the horse for the next movement.

I also stressed how important it is always to keep the communication going. There needs to be a constant conversation going on with you and your horse. If you forget that and just sit there doing nothing, you can't expect your horse to do the right thing, so try to keep the conversation flowing at all times.

LENGTHENING THE STRIDE

Judy had said that Sunnie's medium trot needed to come 'more from behind'. The problem at the moment is that Sunnie sees medium trot as an opportunity to run on to the forehand: as soon as Ann gives him more rein he sets off in this huge trot, getting more and more on the shoulder in the process. So here's what to do.

Ask the horse for medium trot on a circle, so you can keep a better outline. Then as he gives you lengthened strides, just flex his head and neck left and right a little so the neck stays soft. If he isn't charging off with you, then ask for even more.

This made a difference for Sunnie, and his medium trot was much more 'off the shoulder' than it was in the test. I had some more advice: 'When you practise medium trot at home, do it this way, or if you ride it across the diagonal, make sure you only ask for a few strides, then come back to working trot again, so that he doesn't get a chance to charge off.'

A few lengthened strides at a time means Sunnie doesn't have the chance to charge off

Ann lifts her inside hand slightly at a corner to get better inside bend

Ann riding medium walk with a long neck

Working on roundness

I then asked Ann to come on to the left rein. On this rein, Sunnie finds it easier to bend to the inside and consequently he wants to overbend this way, which causes him to fall out through his right shoulder. I told Ann I didn't want her to use the left rein to bend him left, as this just made his nose tilt. Instead, she was to think of turning him with the outside aids. So she must close the right rein against his neck, and use the outside leg to turn, too.

And if he still wasn't round enough? Then she should lower her hands slightly so that the bit rests on the bars of the mouth, to encourage the head and neck to stretch. Then try to keep it, rather than letting the horse drift in and out of it.

Transitions within paces and stopping the leaning

Next I explained how Ann could make the most of Sunnie's great walk. I assured her she should get good marks for his walk, but she had to think of riding the medium walk with a long neck. I don't mean long reins, I mean think of pushing the horse's head and neck away from your body and allowing your hands towards his mouth. Ride with a relaxed leg and open knee, and drop the weight down into your heels.

Finally I had a look at Sunnie's canter. He was too much on the inside rein in canter, so I advised Ann to bend him more to the outside to get the feel of riding him on the outside rein. If you ride a horse with outside bend on both reins, you're still suppling him equally and it stops him leaning on the inside rein.

135

One movement that is often asked for at Novice level is to 'give and retake the reins' in canter. This is a chance to demonstrate to the judge that your horse is in self-carriage – that is, not balancing on his rider's hands. In order to get a good mark for this movement, the horse should stay in the same rhythm, balance and outline.

And you'll really impress the judge if you do it over three strides: over the first stride give the reins away, keep them away for the next stride, and take them back over the third stride. I explained to Ann what the judges are looking for here.

When you ride give and retake, give your hands towards the mouth and get the feeling that the horse is seeking the contact down, rather than seeing it as a great chance to hollow and charge off. You can practise it on a circle to help with this.

Practise giving and retaking the reins on a circle to help the horse reach down into the contact

The retest – Judy Harvey

In their next performance, Ann kept Sunnie more balanced through the first medium trot (he broke to canter in the second), their trot work was rounder, and she rode the test more positively. They finished with a good score of 66.53%.

I considered the test was a big improvement, especially the trot. The canter still needed to be rounder, however, and Sunnie was still inclined to show too much head and neck bend on the left rein.

TIPS AND REMINDERS

- Make sure you ride every step of the way. Don't just leave it to the horse.
- Pick up extra marks by being accurate.
- Think of turning the horse with the inside *and* outside aids, so he doesn't overbend to the inside.
- If he tilts his nose one way, lift the opposite hand up slightly in order to straighten him.
- In the medium trot, practise on a circle, or only do a few steps on a straight line, so the horse doesn't lose his balance and risk breaking to canter.
- Ride deep into the corners; like this you can use them to rebalance the horse, which will help set him up for the next movement.

NOVICE TEST 36

Ann and Sunnie

RETEST RESULTS	
COMMENT	**MARK**
Entry and halt – fairly straight but need to be rounder	6/10
Active and good rhythm in trot on 10m circle right, but fell in a little	7/10
Four-loop serpentine – good bend and balance	8/10
Working trot and 10m circle left – better balance	8/10
Change rein and medium trot strides – could show a little more difference, but good balance	7/10
Halt not square but reinback a little better	5/10
Change rein in medium walk – could be straighter but nice steps	14/20
Working canter left	6/10
20m circle left, give and retake the reins – against hand on circle	5/10
Working canter with medium canter strides – could show more difference	6/10
Working canter and change rein – a bit hollow	6/10
Change of leg through trot – a little against the hand	6/10
20m circle right in working canter, give and retake the reins – give and retake good, but too much bend in neck on circle	6/10
Working canter with medium canter strides	7/10
Working canter and working trot	6/10
Change rein and show some medium trot strides – broke to canter	4/10
10m half-circle left to X, down centre line and halt	7/10
Paces	14/20
Impulsion	12/20
Submission	12/20
Rider's position, seat correctness and effectiveness of aids	14/20
Comment: Well done. Trot much better but in canter still tends to bend neck too much and needs to be rounder	
Total score 173 = 66.53%	

A rounded, more balanced trot improved Ann's score the second time around

Consistency and sensitivity – Carl Hester and Judy Harvey

Aim To assess a horse and rider through Elementary 54 and help them to improve their score

The first test – Judy Harvey

Keith and Limahl rode their very first test together in front of Carl and me – talk about pressure! The pair showed some good medium trot strides, for which I awarded them a seven, as well as a good medium walk and free walk on a long rein. However, their weaker areas were in canter on the left rein, and the shoulder-in. My main comment was that Limahl has lovely paces, but in the test the pair lost marks on a few movements. They were slow to establish shoulder-in, and in left canter, Limahl stiffened to the rider's hand. He broke into trot during the counter-canter movement, and as the canter wasn't re-established, it affected the marks of the next movement. Limahl needs to be more supple, and he needs to accept the bridle as he tends to resist the rider's contact at times.

The pair scored 55% at their first attempt.

HORSE AND RIDER

Keith Robertson runs a livery yard and is an instructor. He was competing at elementary level with his own horse, Cool Ballen, but tragically, the horse died just weeks before the day with Carl and Judy. Keith's instructor, Anna Ross, has kindly lent him one of her horses until Keith's young horse is ready to compete.

Limahl is a 16.1hh, seven-year-old Hanoverian gelding; he is competing at elementary level.

ELEMENTARY TEST 54

Keith and Limahl

FIRST TEST RESULTS	
COMMENT	**MARK**
Enter at collected trot, halt – good halt, could be more active into trot	5/10
10m circle left – a little big, needs to be more supple	6/10
Angle of shoulder-in left not clearly established, uneven steps	5/10
Change rein medium trot, then collected trot – some good strides	7/10
10m circle right, collected trot – resisting, drifting, tense	4/10
Slow to establish shoulder-in right, uneven steps, lost quarters	4/10
Change rein medium trot, collected trot – inaccurate, fell into collected	6/10
Halt then medium walk – halt not quite square	6/10
Medium walk, 20m half-circle in free walk on a long rein, medium walk – some nice steps, could be more consistent in outline	14/20
Working canter left	7/10
Against the hand in 20m circle in medium canter, fell into working canter	5/10
10m half-circle to D return to track at E, counter canter – broke	4/10
Simple change, working canter – wrong canter lead, corrected	4/10
20m circle medium canter, working canter – needs to cover more ground	6/10
10m half-circle to D returning to track at B, counter canter	7/10
Simple change, working canter – against the hand	6/10
Collected trot, down centre line, halt	6/10
Paces	12/20
Impulsion	12/20
Submission	10/20
Rider's position, seat correctness and effectiveness of aids	12/20
Total score 142 = 55%	

Limahl has lovely paces – and shows off his trot down the long side – but tends to tense up on turns

The lesson – Carl Hester

Even rein pressure

I agreed that Limahl was stiff to the right, but I felt this was partly because Keith has a stronger left hand, which prevents the horse bending to the right and being supple on both reins evenly. I suggested an exercise that might help with this: ride a 10m circle on the left rein, but position yourself in outside bend so the horse is flexed to the right. This gives you the chance to use the right leg more strongly to push him around the circle to the left, but it will also have the effect of creating right bend from your leg, rather than from your rein.

As Keith tried this exercise, I advised him not to lean to the right, but just to put weight through his right stirrup.

Developing sensitivity

Limahl tends to get a little dead in the mouth and stuck in one outline. To help with this I suggested Keith gave with the rein and ask the horse to stretch, then bring him back up again into a more collected outline. If he could stretch, collect, stretch, and keep doing this – lots of transitions and flexing work will help to make the horse more supple, and more sensitive to the rein aids.

But while concentrating on the reins for a moment, Keith had forgotten to keep his left leg on, so Limahl's quarters were drifting in to the left. I quickly reminded him not to let his left leg go on holiday, but to hold the horse with his left leg and push the left hind back underneath the tummy.

Limahl is a forward-going horse, and as Keith corrected him, his reaction was to jump forwards into a faster trot, proving that with leg aids there is a fine line between asking for more power, and correcting the horse's position. I said that when a rider is planning to work on positioning, they don't want to create too much impulsion. Make the horse loose first, and then put the energy in.

You need to be able to position the horse's body where you want it, and to have his head and neck loose and flexible, so keep him light in your rein. Then ride his outline up more, change the rein and do the same things on the other rein. Keep varying between stretching down, bending him to either side and riding him up into a more collected outline. Do everything gently and slowly, encouraging him with soft hands.

On the right rein, Keith stretched Limahl to the outside, taking his nose to the left, and gently pushed him out with his right leg, so his hindquarters weren't falling into the circle. I was pleased with Keith's leg aids, and told him that was just what was wanted, to keep the bend with his leg, but to keep his two reins even. I warned him that sometimes he has a blocking left hand, and that he was lifting it higher than his right hand. This creates a strong contact on that side, and that's when the horse becomes rigid.

This is something he needs to keep working on, as it has become a habit to hold on to the left rein.

When on a right circle Keith uses his left rein too much in an attempt to get outside bend

Keith stretches Limahl and then collects him to vary his outline

Riding renvers

From a circle on the right rein, but with outside bend, I asked Keith to ride some renvers (see pp.32–33) down the long side of the arena. To do this, ride the circle, and when you are almost off the track and still in outside bend, half-halt, then keep your left leg on the girth for the horse to bend around. To keep him going forwards, ask for a little flexion with your left rein, and put your right leg on behind the girth to keep his hindquarters on the track and to move him sideways. Your right rein should control the shoulders, and you should look in the direction you are travelling in.

When Keith attempted this, I noted that he was raising his left hand again and crossing it over the withers, and told him to try to keep his hands level with each other. To create more flexion to the left, you need to just open your hand a little rather than pulling the rein up or across.

Lenthening strides

I wanted the pair to try lengthening the trot strides. Limahl showed some nice lengthening in the test, but he still needs to be more sensitive to the rein aids and a little more relaxed on the leg aids, so Keith needs to vary the pace. I suggested he ride him forwards, and then back to collected trot, then ride a small circle, and ride left renvers down the next long side to get him to accept the right rein. He needed to keep asking for lots of change of pace, direction, outline and bend in his schooling.

I reiterated that Keith should aim to get Limahl to relax, while he kept the contact at the same time. The next challenge was to get Limahl to accept Keith's leg aids without reacting too much. With a horse like this it is easy to ride with your legs off, but then when you put your leg on it is too much of a shock to him. So you need to let him feel your ankles against his sides, and ask for lengthening of the strides gradually. While you do this, massage his mouth with the bit and keep it relaxed.

When Keith went into sitting trot, he maintained Limahl in this softer way of going and it looked really nice – the horse looked supple, like you could easily move his neck up or down into a stretch, and he wasn't resisting the contact.

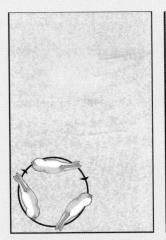

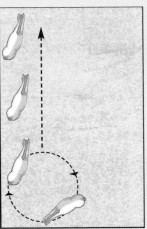

Ride a circle with outside bend: here a right-rein circle with left bend

As you come off the track at the top of the circle, continue along the long side

The pair in renvers – ideally Limahl should be more supple in the left bend

Limahl is not at quite the correct angle in his shoulder-in – it should be performed at 35 degrees to the track. (Inset) Carl demonstrates the correct angle for shoulder-in on three distinct tracks

Making good angles

I then asked Keith to ride a circle to the left but with outside bend, and from the circle to ride a shoulder-in (see pp.22–24) down the centre line. For this you want to have an angle of about 35 degrees and keep it consistently until you finish the movement. Sometimes these movements seem to shock Limahl a little, so I told Keith to be very clear with his aids.

Keeping the canter

To prepare for some work in canter, Keith rode another circle, asked for renvers to lighten Limahl on the left rein, and then made a transition to canter.

I suggested that to improve the flow of the canter, he should keep a bend in his knee and get used to opening his shoulders. He also needed to keep his legs in contact with Limahl's sides, otherwise he would lose the canter, just like he did in the test.

Just then Limahl did break from canter. I advised Keith to loosen him up, circle, prepare him with a tap from the inside leg, and then ask for canter again. I warned him that on the right rein, his left side was still the problem, so not to let the horse stiffen on it – to give him a little kick if he dropped the contact more than once – he needed to be on the aids. I suggested Keith ride a little renvers, as this seemed to work well as a correction for Limahl, then to straighten him up and try again.

The counter canter caused a problem for Keith in the test as Limahl broke to trot as he was returning to the track. However, it should be possible to keep the canter going by consistently keeping the inside leg on, and by pushing the horse towards the track with the outside leg.

You also need to keep your weight in the inside seatbone when you ride counter canter, because this will help the horse to maintain his balance throughout the movement.

After a few attempts Keith managed to keep Limahl in canter. I wanted the horse to relax again, so asked them to canter on the right rein and for Keith to maintain the softness on the bit while keeping his leg on Limahl's side.

Keith maintains Limahl in counter canter, although the horse is being a little resistant

HOW TO RIDE COUNTER CANTER RIGHT

1. On the right rein, establish a good working or collected canter.
2. Half-halt to balance the horse, before riding a half 10m circle at the corner.
3. Ride towards the track at a shallow angle, but aim to arrive at the track well before you get to the corner.
4. Keep the right leg on the girth to maintain bend, but also to push the horse towards the track.
5. Keep the weight on your inside seatbone.
6. Use the right rein to keep the horse's flexion to the right.
7. Keep the left leg behind the girth to maintain right canter lead.
8. Use the left rein to control the horse's shoulders and keep him in balance.

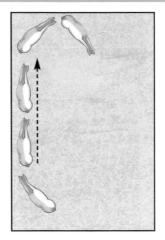

Establish right canter

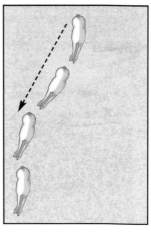

Return to the track maintaining right canter lead

By contrast, a relaxed, soft and supple transition into canter

Once a good canter was established I suggested that Keith should give and retake the reins. Limahl maintained a soft outline through the give and retake, and after a good transition to trot, I was pleased to see a ground-covering trot stride that had a real swing to it.

Keith was enjoying this new confident partnership and the work his horse was producing, too. I asked for a shoulder-in, which they performed well, and I praised Keith. However, there was just one more thing: he now had the confidence to tell Limahl to do shoulder-in, but he also needed to finish it positively too. It was very nice, but I told him he should also remember to look where he was going, and not down at his horse's neck!

The retest – Judy Harvey

The pair finished their lesson on a good note, and then had a rest before riding the dressage test again, with myself as judge. This time I was pleased to see that Keith rode the shoulder-in to the left with a clear, established angle, and I gave him a mark of seven; I also gave him sevens for his early trot work and for the walk movement.

Their shoulder-in to the right was not so good, as Limahl's quarters were in at the start and the angle varied a little; however, they did improve their previous mark by two points! Unfortunately the pair lost the canter in the second test at the same place they had lost it in the first. Nevertheless, Keith was quicker to re-establish the canter so they didn't lose quite as many marks here.

I also commented that they needed to show more difference in the medium canter from the working canter; and the horse was still a little against the hand at times. However, I felt the quality of the paces had improved, as had Keith's position and his use of the aids, so they collected more marks in this section, too. Despite their mistakes in canter, the pair still managed to improve their mark to a very respectable 62%.

At the end of the test I congratulated Keith and told him it was a lot better! The horse looked more supple, and he wasn't resisting the contact quite so much. However, I suggested Keith should be careful when asking Limahl to go more forwards, to help him keep his balance through the corners.

ELEMENTARY TEST 54

Keith and Limahl

RETEST RESULTS	
COMMENT	**MARK**
Enter at collected trot and halt	7/10
10m circle left	7/10
Shoulder-in left	7/10
Change rein medium trot then collected – could cover more ground in medium	6/10
10m circle right, collected trot – slight loss of balance	6/10
Shoulder-in right – quarters in at the start, but the angle varied	6/10
Down centre line change rein in medium trot, collected trot	7/10
Halt then medium walk – a little heavy on rein but very square	7/10
Medium walk, 20m half-circle in free walk on a long rein, medium walk	14/20
Working canter left – a little tense	5/10
20m circle left in medium canter, working canter – needs to show clearer difference, against the hand at E	5/10
10m half-circle to D return to track at E, counter canter – broke, inaccurate	4/10
Simple change of leg, working canter – against the hand	5/10
20m circle medium canter, working canter – needs to show more difference	6/10
10m half-circle to D returning to track at B, counter canter	6/10
Simple change of leg, working canter	6/10
Collected trot, down centre line, halt	7/10
Paces	14/20
Impulsion	12/20
Submission	10/20
Rider's position, seat correctness and effectiveness of aids	14/20
Comment: Well done, trot work was better but circle left needs to be more supple	
Total score 161 = 62%	

Keith and Limahl's partnership has improved enormously

KEITH'S VERDICT

So what did Keith feel he'd gained from the session? 'I've learned I can ride the horse more positively and feel I am going somewhere, although I've got to work on getting him rounder and softer.'

SITTING TROT – BEREITER HERWIG, LAURA BECHTOLSHEIMER, CHRISTOPHER BARTLE

What are the benefits of sitting trot? How do you sit to trot? How do you train your horse to accept this work? Three top riders give their opinions.

Bereiter Herwig – Spanish Riding School, Vienna

Sitting trot is important for all our collected trot work, because you have more even control over your hands and legs – and of course, your seat – than in rising trot. When you are learning sitting trot it is best to find a horse that is very even in rhythm, because you must not hold on by squeezing with your knees, which might happen with a bouncy horse if you feel you're being thrown out of balance. At the School, cadets work on the lunge for as long as it takes them to develop a truly independent seat. This allows them to concentrate on their own body and the movements of the horse, without worrying about controlling the horse. Constant training is absolutely necessary to perfect the seat – you have to give your body the chance to learn to move with the horse, and this takes time.

Warming up the horse or cooling it down, we use rising trot to give the horse the opportunity to warm up or relax/cool down his muscles. When it comes to serious dressage work, such as transitions and lateral work, it's necessary to sit, as it is whenever we do collected work.

We start training our horses relatively late – they are approximately four years old when they come to us. After a couple of months of simple training, we gently start the sitting trot, keeping in mind that there are differences from horse to horse. You can feel whether or not the horse accepts the sitting trot and if so, you can continue doing it. It is important that the rider really can sit into the horse and is not bouncing around, because then he won't harm the horse's back.

Laura Bechtolsheimer – British Dressage National Champion

Sitting trot is useful when asking for transitions and, when you reach a higher level, doing harder movements. It also helps to keep the horse on the aids. Without a strong seat, you can't sit to the trot.

Sit in balance with your back straight, elbows at right angles and hanging loosely by your side, with the hands in a forward position. The hips must be loose and swing to the movement of the horse, with the legs hanging softly against the horse's side. Try to sit comfortably, but with enough tension in the body to maintain your position – but avoid doing a belly dance! Have a good contact in the hand without balancing on your horse's mouth – and no grippy knees! If you grip with your knees, you'll push yourself out of the saddle, when you need to sit 'into' your bum.

Laura Bechtolsheimer and Douglas Dorsey

The better your seat position, the easier it is to ride sitting trot. This rider has a balanced position which allows her to move softly with the horse

If you have a horse with an uncomfortable trot, the only thing you can do is try to go with the movement! Although my Grand Prix horse, Douglas Dorsey, swings along and is quite bouncy, he's quite slow which makes it easier to adjust to sitting trot. And what's interesting is that Douglas, even with his big, elevated trot, is easier to sit to than some of my event ponies ever were!

Christopher Bartle

The basis of a good sitting trot is for the rider to have good posture and to stay in good balance. Good posture involves the core muscles, those of the lower back and abdomen. If the back muscles are well developed but the abdominal ones are not, the result is a hollow back. Balance depends on the vertical alignment of the head, neck and spine of the rider above the seatbones. When riding on a circle, lateral balance requires that the rider sits slightly to the inside of the saddle in order to counteract the natural tendency to slip to the outside.

When I'm teaching I say 'the more you bounce, the better they go'. This is because I see many riders being self-conscious about their sitting trot so they grip, or absorb the movement through the waist. This leads to the 'head nod', which reminds me of a chicken running across a farmyard! With a very bouncy horse, lean back a bit more. To make the horse less bouncy over time, do more lateral work, especially leg yielding and then shoulder-in. This will teach him to be more elastic through the back and to engage and flex the hindleg instead of pushing with it.

Christopher Bartle and Word Perfect

Practising trotting without stirrups improves your position and helps you to master sitting trot

Developing expression – Carl Hester and Judy Harvey

Aim To assess a horse and rider through Medium Test 71 and help them to improve their score

---

HORSE AND RIDER

Yolande Eldridge, a teacher at Amery Hill School in Hampshire, has owned her lovely horse Talisker for seven years. They enjoy competing in dressage and have worked up the grades to Medium level.

Talisker is a 17.1hh, 13-year-old, Irish Sport Horse. Yolande was devastated when, six weeks prior to the lesson, Tali was struck with a mystery virus that left him in intensive care. However, he has made a remarkable recovery.

The first test – Judy Harvey

Under test conditions, Yolande and Tali performed most of the movements quite well, especially those in collected canter. However, their weaker areas were the lateral movements – half-pass and travers. I had to mark them down on these movements as Tali lacked bend in the travers, and needed better positioning in the half-pass. In addition, the horse's steps became irregular and less active in the lateral work.

I also felt that Yolande wasn't asking enough from Tali in the medium canter, especially as the rest of the horse's canter work was good.

In the test, Tali works with a short, tight neck in extended walk

MEDIUM TEST **71**

Yolande and Tali

FIRST TEST RESULTS	
COMMENT	**MARK**
Enter at collected trot, halt – on forehand into halt, good move off	6/10
Two 10m half-circles – overshot first half-circle	6/10
Travers – needs more bend	5/10
Change rein at medium trot, collected trot	6/10
Half-pass right – lacking bend and angle, irregular steps to start	4/10
Two 10m half-circles – good bend and rhythm	7/10
Travers – needs more bend	5/10
Change rein at medium trot, collected trot	6/10
Half-pass right, track right – clearer positioning needed	5/10
Extended then collected walk – walk rhythm varying, tight in neck	5/10
Collected canter left – good	7/10
Track left, collected canter – good	7/10
Half-pass left, track left – needs to maintain activity	6/10
Medium canter, collected canter – not enough for medium canter	5/10
Simple change of leg to change rein – good balance and transitions	7/10
Collected canter – rather tense	6/10
Half-pass right, track right – needs more bend, not enough angle	4/10
Medium, then collected canter – not enough difference shown	6/10
Simple change – walk steps not clear, tending to jog	5/10
Collected canter, collected trot	6/10
Down centre line, halt, reinback, collected trot	7/10
Halt, leave arena on long rein	7/10
Paces	12/20
Impulsion	10/20
Submission	12/20
Rider's position, seat correctness and effectiveness of aids	12/20
Comment: Some better moments in canter, but half-pass needs some work now	
Total score 179 = 57.7%	

n walk, Tali's rhythm varied a little and was not secure. In the extended walk, I would have liked to have seen the horse stretching down into the contact with less tightness in his neck and more swing in his back, and tracking up better with his hindlegs.

After their test, Carl made these comments to Yolande: 'Tali is impressive and has a good outline. However, you look like you are working quite hard, and yet he lacks a little expression. He needs more energy, and this will help to improve the half-passes and travers'.

The lesson – Carl Hester

Creating energy

At the beginning of the lesson, I asked Yolande to ride some medium trot while keeping a good contact. I suggested she try to keep her hands still, as sometimes she allowed the contact to become a little fragile.

I instruct Yolande to think every corner, and if Tali feels sluggish, to push on into medium trot and then collect again.

Under my direction, Yolande then rode medium trot to collected trot, back to medium, back again to collected and finally into canter.

I explained that riding lots of transitions, within and between paces, helps to get the horse connected and more expressive. When you ask him to go forwards, use a tapping aid with your legs rather than a squeeze. You can then take your leg off him and he should maintain the pace – otherwise you end up working harder than him.

Interestingly, when Yolande followed my advice and gave Tali a little kick with her leg, he bucked! I told her that was a sign that he's normally behind her leg.

To continue to improve Tali's response to Yolande's aids, I asked her to do more transitions. I also suggested that when she reached the corners she should keep the flow, and open and close her inside leg through the turn to allow him to reach into his stride.

I also observed that she has a tendency to hold back when she sits to the trot, which can restrict the energy in the horse's stride. If this happens, when you ride down the long sides, start in sitting trot, then half-way along rise to the trot to encourage forward energy. Sit again before the corner, and then canter. These exercises – lengthening the strides in trot and canter – really help the paces to become more expressive.

Yolande alternates working in sitting trot with rising trot to avoid restricting the energy in Talisker's stride

Walking like a racehorse

An area where Yolande had lost marks in the test was the walk. I explained it is important to get a good mark because although the walk is a basic movement, it is worth double marks, and it also affects the paces mark you are given in the collectives, so you need to do it well.

When Yolande has to push Tali in the walk, it loses its natural swing and rhythm. And when he is short in the neck his steps become irregular. So I advised her to be sure to allow him to almost poke his nose out and stretch forwards and down, by relaxing herself. When she grips, he shortens: Yolande has to think 'nose out like a racehorse', and then he'll overtrack.

Under my guidance, Yolande and Tali produce a better outline and rhythm in extended walk

Positive riding results in increasing expression from Talisker

Getting impulsion in canter

I wanted Yolande to ask for more impulsion in the medium canter, which would produce a more powerful, ground-covering stride in Tali. To help with this, I asked her to rise to the trot to get Tali going forwards, and only sit to the trot just before asking for canter. Once in canter, I told Yolande to take her legs away from his sides, then put the leg on to ask for medium canter, and I encouraged her to go with the forward movement. To collect, I told Yolande to bring her body up and back. After a successful attempt I commented that it was nice to see him almost running away with her – and how expressive he looked!

Developing bend

Once Yolande and Tali had relaxed into their walk, I started to help them with the lateral movements. In their test, Judy had commented that every lateral movement they performed lacked bend (or correct positioning). For example, in travers, the horse should be bent in the direction in which he is travelling, with his inside foreleg and outside hindleg on the same track, and his inside hindleg on an inside track, which Tali tended not to do.

To work on this, I asked Yolande to bring Tali's head to the inside in walk, and then to use her outside leg to bend him round. I kept my finger on Tali's shoulder so as to prevent him from moving his shoulders in.

I then talked Yolande through an exercise from travers into a half-pass (see pp.26–27 and 30–1): she was to carefully bend his nose to the inside again, and then lighten the rein. You make the horse bend first, then use your outside leg to ask him to travel diagonally across the school in half-pass. As I walked backwards, I told her to flex him and then release – I needed to see his two eyes on me – but think about travelling along a diagonal line to the side.

Yolande and Tali practised their half-passes, but on occasion Tali seemed to get stuck. I advised Yolande not to allow his quarters to come too far over and lead the movement, because that was when he got stuck. Let the quarters follow, but not trail. That piece of advice seemed to strike a chord with Yolande, as she then rode a very accurate half-pass.

I congratulated them, and said it was the first real half-pass he'd done that day!

Tali's head should be facing me in this attempt at travers

I stop Tali from moving his shoulders in

Tali's angle in travers is now a little better, but he stills needs more bend

I demonstrate how it's done!

TIPS FOR HALF-PASS

- Bend the horse to the inside, then release the rein pressure.
- Use the inside leg to keep the bend and the outside leg to create sideways movement.
- Keep the horse's head facing in the direction of travel.
- Imagine travelling along a line that is diagonal to the side of the school.
- If your horse feels stuck (loses the rhythm and impulsion) it might be because his hindlegs are leading – use less outside leg.

Putting it all together

After the success with the half-passes, I was keen that Yolande didn't lose the expression that had been created at the beginning of the session.

I reminded her to think about every corner, and if Tali felt sluggish again, to push on into medium trot or canter and then collect back again. You need to be loose and light with your lower leg, and avoid gripping, which suppresses the horse's paces. For lateral work, don't keep riding half-passes to make it better, use the side of the arena and ask for a little travers.

I suggested she get someone to stand at the top of the school on the long side to check they could see both of Tali's eyes, so she knew she had the right amount of bend – too much, and the quarters will struggle to stay on an inside track.

MEDIUM TEST **71**

Yolande and Tali

RETEST RESULTS

COMMENT	MARK
Enter at collected trot, halt, track left	7/10
Two 10m half-circles	7/10
Travers – lost angle early	6/10
Change rein at medium trot, collected trot – became a little hollow	6/10
Half-pass right – needs more bend	6/10
Two 10m half-circles	7/10
Travers – needs more suppleness	6/10
Change rein at medium trot, collected trot	6/10
Half-pass right, track right – more bend needed	5/10
Extended then collected walk – could be more consistently forward	6/10
Collected canter left	7/10
Track left, collected canter	7/10
Half-pass left, track left	7/10
Medium canter, collected canter – could be more forward	6/10
Simple change of leg to change rein – a little lazy into canter	6/10
Collected canter	7/10
Half-pass right, track right – trailing	5/10
Medium, then collected canter – a little lazy	6/10
Simple change of leg to change rein	7/10
Collected canter, collected trot	7/10
Down centre line, halt, reinback, collected trot	8/10
Halt, leave arena on long rein	8/10
Paces	14/20
Impulsion	12/20
Submission	12/20
Rider's position, seat correctness and effectiveness of aids	14/20
Comment: Well done – the half-passes are improving and because he was more engaged, your halts were better	
Total score 201 = 68.4%	

The retest – Judy Harvey

After a break, Yolande and Tali rode their Medium Test 71 again. This time, although their travers and half-passes still needed more bend, I felt they had improved. And I added that because Tali had become more engaged in his work, this also improved the halts – so for those I gave them two marks of eight!

I also gave Tali a higher mark for his paces in the collectives, indicating that the walk work had improved, too. The pair scored a very respectable 64.8% – not bad for a horse who was fighting for his life just six weeks earlier!

YOLANDE'S VERDICT

Yolande was delighted with her lesson from Carl and observations from Judy: 'I realized in the half-pass that I'm starting with too much from the hindquarters, and I've been trying to get him to look into the school for the travers, instead of straight ahead up the long side. I understand now that in half-pass I need to turn his front end first, and then ask for sideways steps, so he has time to cross over.

'I've also learnt not to try so hard, otherwise I tend to block his movement. Carl made me do less – and I got more from Tali!'

By doing less, Yolande has persuaded Talisker to give her more

Acknowledgments

The text in this book has been complied from articles that originally appeared in *Horse & Rider* magazine. The articles were written by the following people, with help from the team at *Horse & Rider*:

Nicky Barrett was the 2002 National Dressage Champion, taking the title just weeks after undergoing surgery on her back. In fact, Nicky almost didn't ride her winning test, due to the pain that she was suffering at the time.

Christopher Bartle has an impressive track record. He is the highest placed British team member in the history of Olympic Dressage (he finished 6th), and has proved to be one of the best event riders in the world, winning Badminton in 1998 with Word Perfect. Chris currently trains the German eventing team.

Richard Davison was the British National Dressage Champion in 2003 with Ballaseyr Royale, he won a team silver medal at the European Championships in 1993, and was a member of the bronze medal-winning team in 2003. Gill Davison (Richard's wife) helps him with riding, training and competing the horses.

Emile Faurie has represented Great Britain at two Olympic Games, three World Equestrian Games and four European Championships, as well as winning the British National Dressage Championships on two occasions.

Judy Harvey is a List One British Dressage judge, which means she can judge to Grand Prix level.

Carl Hester is one of the UK's best dressage riders. He has 40 national dressage titles, he's been National Dressage Champion four times and, riding Escapado, was the highest placed UK rider at the Athens Olympics.

Lee Pearson OBE has an impressive competition record – not only has he won six Paralympic gold medals, five World and three European Championships, he has also taken a national title against able-bodied riders at the British National Dressage Championships. He has also won the BBC Midlands' Sports Personality of the Year.

Tina Sederholm has ridden and trained horses and riders up to international standard in three-day eventing for the last 20 years. She is the author of *Unlock Your Riding Talent* and *Secrets of the Top Equestrian Trainers*, both published by David & Charles.

Amy Stovold was catapulted into the limelight when she and her 17hh Holstein stallion, Lenski, won the Rhinegold six-year-old Potential Dressage Horse Championship in 2003 with a massive 81.8%. They then went on to become the Medium Restricted UK National Dressage champions in 2004.

A freelance dressage trainer based at her own yard in West Sussex, Amy has horses competing from Novice to Intermediare.

Perry Wood divides his time between teaching horses and riders, and helping corporate executives learn about communication and leadership through interaction with horses. He has studied with classical riding masters and translates their teachings into something easily usable by any rider. He has written several books including *Real Riding*, *Secrets of the People Whisperer* and *How to Create the Perfect Riding Horse*.